War 1812:

Battle of New Orleans

Michael Aye

Published by Boson Books

An imprint of Bitingduck Press
Formerly an imprint of C&M Online Media, Inc.

eISBN 978-1-938463-47-1

© 2017 Michael A. Fowler All rights reserved. No part of this book may be reproduced, stored in a retrieval system, or transmitted in any form, including mechanical, electric, photocopy, recording or otherwise, without the prior written permission of the author.

For information contact
Bitingduck Press, LLC
Montreal • Altadena
notifications@bitingduckpress.com
http://www.bitingduckpress.com
Cover art: Mike Benton

Author's note

This book is a work of fiction with a historical backdrop. I have taken liberties with historical figures, ships, and time frames to blend in with my story. Therefore, this book is not a reflection of actual historical events.

Books by Michael Aye

The Reaper, Book One, The Fighting Anthonys

HMS SeaWolf, Book Two, The Fighting Anthonys

Barracuda, Book Three, The Fighting Anthonys

SeaHorse, Book Four, The Fighting Anthonys

Peregrine, Book Five, The Fighting Anthonys

Trident, Book Six, The Fighting Anthonys

Leopard, Book Seven, The Fighting Anthonys

Remember the Raisin, Book One, War 1812

Battle at Horseshoe Bend, Book Two, War 1812

The Pyrate, Book 1, The Pyrates

This book is dedicated

to all our American Veterans. I salute and honor you. God bless you and God bless America.

In 1814, we took a little trip
Along with Colonel Jackson down the mighty Mississippi
We took a little bacon and we took a little beans
And we caught the bloody British in the town of New Orleans
We fired our guns and the British kept a coming
There wasn't nigh as many as there was awhile ago
Fired once more and they began to running
On down the Mississippi to the Gulf of Mexico

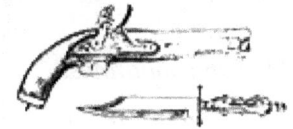

Prologue

"GUNFIRE...I HEAR IT, BANTY. Better go down and tell the Captain," Johannes Ewers, Master of the Marque, Seafire, said to his seaman. Johannes and the rest of the crew were still trying to get used to their new found status. Still pirates, some would say of the privateers. Pirates, but with a license, a legitimacy. 'The old days are gone,' the captain, Cooper Cain had said. 'We can change with it and openly enjoy it or we can continue our course as free men of the sea and soon we'll die.' All but a few had decided to change and stay with the captain. The crew was basically the same as before. Titles, ranks, that sort of thing had changed, mostly in name but now they could come and go without worry. Well, they could in America. They'd still have to worry about the British. Yet, that was not much of concern. They'd never got caught, and most felt with Cooper Cain and Mac, short for David MacArthur, being the lucky souls they were, getting caught was not high on the crew's list of concern.

"There to larboard," Spurlock, the gunner, said. "Flashes, I see flashes from the guns."

The sun had just faded over the horizon on a cloudless night. The moon hung low and was nearly full, making the deck nearly as bright as day.

Mac, now the first officer, was on deck before the captain. "Bring her about, Mr. Ewers, you know Coop...er... the captain is going to want a closer look."

"Aye."

The bosun's pipe shrilled out and hands flooded the deck to change tack and bear down on the sea fight. The evolution was in progress when

Captain Cooper Cain came on deck. Ewers made his report with only a few questions from the captain.

"What do you think?" Cain asked, speaking to Mac and Johannes.

"It figures to be one of ours fighting one of theirs," Johannes replied.

"Simply put, but spot on, I'd say," Mac added.

As Seafire ran down on the combatants, Cain waited patiently. By the sound of the cannons echoing across the water, the ships were not that big. Smaller than a frigate, surely. Banty had been sent aloft with a night glass. They were much closer now and the firing was lessening. Somebody had won the battle or was close to it.

Banty shouted down, "British sloop o' war has taken what looks to be an American merchant brig."

Seizing this information, Cain quickly ordered his first officer, "Man the guns, Mac, let's see if we can give yonder sloop a taste of the same medicine she is giving our American friend."

Seafire's deck was now alive, not with drums and fifes of a naval war ship, but with the fiddler laying down a spicy little jig. In a little over four minutes, the ship was reported ready for battle. Not bad for nighttime, Cooper thought. He knew that they could shave a little time off if the situation demanded it, though.

"Deck thar," Banty yelled down. "They've spied us and they's making to come about."

Too late, Cain thought. "Fire as you bear, Mac! Let's give them a taste of Seafire's metal."

The deck vibrated as the gun trucks rumbled home. Night vision was then gone as orange flames belched forth, lighting up the night sky. An entire deafening broadside was let loose. Quickly the gunners laid into their guns and another broadside boomed out. Not quite in unison but one right after the other.

"She's struck," Banty yelled down.

"We did it, Captain," Mac said, turning and smiling to his captain. "We surprised them, Coop. They didn't even get a shot off."

"Aye," Ewers joined in. "Our gunners know their business."

"Well then, let's go look at our prize," Cain answered.

"Prizes, Captain, that's a British flag flying over the brig."

"Yes, then let's see to our prizes and hopefully we can get them to Savannah unmolested."

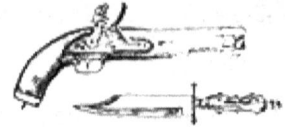

CHAPTER ONE

Reuben, the son of Colonel Lee's overseer rushed into the yard out of breath. He had come straight from Thunderbolt, where he had been sent on an errand for Mama Lee. The news in Thunderbolt was so exciting, the lad forgot about the errand and rushed back to tell everyone. Colonel Lee and his sons, Jonah and Moses, sat on the side porch in the shade of a huge oak tree.

"Colonel Lee…Colonel Lee!"

"What is it, Reuben?"

"That Captain Cain done come down the river wid two ships he done took. One is a Redcoat war ship and dat odder one is the *Lady Amelia*."

Colonel Lee recognized the ship's name. She was a ship from Saint Mary. Her owner and captain had been warned about trying to outguess the British and sneak past the British blockade. Captain Harvey had been lucky in the past and now it seems he had pushed his luck one too many times.

"What about her captain?" the colonel asked the boy.

"Captain, which captain, Colonel?"

"The *Lady Amelia's* captain," Lee clarified in an aggravated voice.

"He be dead. Him and Mr. Krause."

"Damnation," Lee swore. Both had been good men, foolish but good men.

"Let's ride into town," Jonah suggested.

Moses nodded his head in agreement, "I'll get our horses."

"Yes, do that," Colonel Lee said. "I'll go tell Mama Lee that we'll be back soon."

"I 'spect I better ride wid you," Reuben muttered.

"Why?" Moses asked. "You just came from town."

"Yes, suh, I did, but I forgot to pick up Mama Lee's sewing things."

"Yes, you'd better come with us before mama learns you forgot. Otherwise, you won't be able to sit a horse or anything else for a week."

Reuben swallowed hard. "I'll walk down to the stables wid you, Moses."

Jonah and Moses laughed. "He's trying to stay out of sight," Jonah chuckled.

A CROWD STOOD AT THE river's edge and watched as British prisoners were marched off *HMS Spitfire*, of eighteen guns— a flush-deck, ship-rigged sloop-of-war. It was a significant prize that should be expedited through the prize court. The merchant ship, *Lady Amelia*, would take a little more time. With the captain being half-owner, her other owners would be contacted and informed of the deaths of Captain Harvey and First Mate Krause.

Seeing his friends on horseback behind the gathered crowd, Captain Cooper Cain walked up to where they sat on their horses. "Colonel, Jonah, Moses! You all look well."

"And you, son. I see fortune has smiled upon you once more," Colonel Lee replied.

"Aye, once Mac gets the prisoners secured we could meet and share a tankard. Mac will buy, I'm sure."

The colonel smiled, "Generous of you, Captain."

"Especially with Mac's money," Jonah laughed.

The group had been friends for a few years now. When Eli Taylor had brought Cooper Cain and Mac to Savannah a while back, it had been Jonah and Moses who had acted as guides for the overland trip back to New Orleans. A friendship had been forged on the trail, and had grown with time.

TANKARDS OF ALE SAT on the smooth oak table as Cooper and Mac told of capturing the *Spitfire*. During the narrative a man in buckskins walked up to the table. Hat in hand, the man's coal black hair hung down to his shoulders. Waiting to be recognized before he spoke, the man stood patiently.

Seeing a shadow cross the table, Colonel Lee looked up. "May we help you, friend?"

Nodding, the man spoke in a slow southern drawl that reminded Jonah of Captain Clay Gessling, a Kentucky volunteer, who Moses and he had teamed up with fighting the British in the Northwest. The man asked, "Would one of you be Jonah Lee?"

"I'm Jonah, what can I do for you?"

"Got a letter for you." Reaching under his buckskin shirt, the man pulled an envelope out and handed it to Jonah.

Jonah took the crumpled envelope and tore it open.

Dear Jonah,

I hope this finds you and Moses well. I understand from Major Hampton that you continue in our righteous fight to rid our homeland of foreign invaders. As has been mentioned in the past, I've had feelers out attempting to repay your kindness and support of me by trying to locate your Anastasia. Luck, it seems, may have finally come our way. It has been reported to me a group of trappers have with them two women. One is an Indian, but the other is said to speak in a French accent. It is also said that while the woman is not bound, she is not free to go as she pleases. The group's movements have been followed as they have made their way down the Natchez Trace. They were last seen at Hawkins Stand but were overheard saying the plan was to travel to Jackson, Mississippi on the Pearle River. The man I sent with this letter is a trusted man who knows the area and people well. His name is Donnie Hall. His son's name is Tim, and they travel with a dried-up sinner known as Scrap Isreal. If

I learn anything more, word will be left at certain points known by Donnie and Scrap.

The letter was signed, "Your comrade in arms, Richard M. Johnson."

"I'll be damned," Jonah swore, as he handed the letter to his father to read, while Moses and Cooper looked on from each side.

At the Battle of the Thames, Colonel Johnson had been wounded several times. The Indian leader, Tecumseh had taken aim at the colonel. Jonah had been quick to draw a bead on Tecumseh and shot the chief, killing him. Johnson had shot as well but, weak from his wounds, the colonel had been unable to bring his rifle to bear. His shot went harmlessly into the ground. Johnson knew that Jonah had just saved his life. Yet another man, a Kentucky volunteer, who was on the opposite side of the colonel's horse, heard the shot and saw Tecumseh fall. The Kentuckian yelled out, 'The colonel just killed Tecumseh.' Quickly the word was spread through the troops. Although the colonel never said he was the one to shoot the Indian leader, neither did he deny it.

MAJOR JAMES HAMPTON, ONE of the president's spies, had advised Jonah to let Johnson continue to be known as the man who killed Tecumseh. 'Johnson is a man of means and has political ambition. Were one to keep silent about the Tecumseh shooting, that person would gain a powerful friend and ally.'

Jonah and Moses had remained close-mouthed, and Hampton's words of having an ally seemed to be coming true. Looking at the date on the letter, Jonah gave a sigh. The letter was weeks old, and for him to reach Jackson would take many more weeks. The men could be anywhere by the time he got there.

Seeing the despair on Jonah's face, Cooper asked, "Is there a problem, Jonah?"

"Yes, unfortunately, it's likely to take a month to get to Jackson. Anything could happen in that time...just when I feel so close."

"A month," Cooper repeated. "I think not. Colonel, would you send to Savannah for one of Captain Taylor's solicitors. We will turn the captured ships' disposal over to Eli and his group. Be ready to sail on the morning tide, Jonah. We will have you in the area in a week or so if the winds hold true."

Grasping his friend's hand, Jonah smiled. "You are a good friend, Cooper."

"I know what being in love is all about," Cooper said and winked. "I'll be off to see Maddy now."

Donnie Hall, the buckskin attired scout, didn't gleam with the joy Jonah had shown. Colonel Johnson had told him to go assist Jonah but he didn't let on there'd be getting into a boat. Not a boat that went beyond the sight of land, no how. *Wonder what Timmy and Scrap will say when they learn the plan? Liable to take off*, he reckoned. Loading his pipe, Donnie decided he'd collect the two and all their trappings but wouldn't let on anything else until it was too late.

Realizing that Donnie was still standing at the table, Colonel Lee addressed him, "Go get your men and horses, Mr. Hall. We'll ride out to our place. We will keep your horses quartered until you return."

"Thank you," Hall said, as he walked away.

Once the scout was out of sight, Moses asked, "Do you think Mr. Hall is well? He looked peaked...pale and peaked when he left. Don't reckon he's sick, do you?"

"I didn't notice," Jonah replied.

"Probably wore out from the trail," the colonel threw out. "A few days at sea with clean air and rest will do him good."

"Aye," Moses said with a smile, using the nautical lingo he'd picked up from Cooper and Mac.

"Don't reckon it was the thought of going to sea, do you?" Mac asked.

"Some fear the sea. More likely he got a good look at Moses' mug. He'd scare anyone." Jonah's words were greeted by a thump to the side of his head. "Dang, Moses."

Shaking his head, the colonel looked at Cooper and Mac, "I thought my sons had matured, but it's kids they are. Keep your cat handy, Captain… and don't be afraid to use it on these two."

"I don't think it will come to that, Colonel, but it's always close and I have a couple who know how to use it."

With a nudge, Moses asked, "Hear that Jonah, that ain't no four-legged kitty they's talking about."

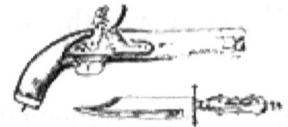

CHAPTER TWO

Seafire glided along the peaceful Wilmington River. Men went about their duties as quietly as possible.

"Wassaw Sound, dead ahead," Johannes Ewers whispered to the first officer. Mac nodded his response.

British warships rarely patrolled the sound; instead they spent most of their time plying back and forth off Tybee Roads, the entrance to the Savannah River and to the city of Savannah, Georgia. Cooper stood on the quarterdeck, while Mac was standing by the wheel and Johannes was nearby.

"It's a wonder to me why the British fail to patrol the Wilmington River and Wassaw Sound," Johannes whispered.

"Doubt they have an up to date chart. They likely don't know how navigable it is. Or is there such a shortage of ships that it forced the local naval commander to make the decision to closely guard one route to the Atlantic Ocean and ignore the other?" Cooper replied. The British had been lucky more than once and swept down on a blockade runner coming out of Savannah. Luckily, *Seafire* had now made it into the Atlantic, so Captain Taylor's route was still unknown.

The hour after dawn made the horizon seem so near that Jonah felt like he could just reach out and touch it. On the surface, the limited area of vision lay empty. Long gray rollers that crashed against *Seafire's* hull seemed endless. As each wave swept under the keel, the ship rolled back and forth. Johnson's man, Scrap Israel, was pale. His tobacco stained grey whiskers hid the green of seasickness but his eyes were glassy. Being topside, as Moses had recommended, had helped. Perhaps it was the cooler, freshness of the air...the air and the wind. The only thing now that caused the bile to boil was the ship's motion. It would rise on the crest of a wave and then sink into the trough, roll, and then rise again. All around him on the deck and aloft, men went about their duties seemingly oblivious to the ship's infernal motion.

Scrap was not a seaman. But even to a landsman, the distant sky looked menacing. Yet in spite of the hazardous look of the sky, the ship continued on course. Were the Gods of the sea laughing at his discomfort? Had they decided what fun it'd be to see him cast his stomach contents into the sea, or were they demons of his past deeds finally catching up with him? Demons deciding to torture him while he had no place to run. It was then upon him... he couldn't hold back. He spewed... and spewed again... and again. They'd won, but surprisingly he felt better. Would they let him be now? Hopefully, he could rest now, if not, he'd show the old imp what for, once they reached land. *Enjoy this victory now, old son,* he thought. *You'll see Scrap Israel strut again once dry land was reached.*

SEAFIRE'S JOURNEY SOUTH WAS uneventful other than for a couple of squalls. No ships of any size had been sighted and now they were in the Florida Straits. The morrow would see them in the Gulf of Mexico. How long had it been? Nearly three years since he was first taken aboard the pirate ship, *Raven*. It was his first foray into the Gulf of Mexico with Eli Taylor. It was mostly fond memories but not all. Yet it was with Eli that he'd met the Lees and they'd become close friends. Jonah was known to be the president's man. He'd been sent to key places, key battles as the president's eyes and ears. He, in fact, was to hook back up with Jackson in Mobile. But that would have to wait. It was time for Jonah to worry about Anastasia. But Cooper Cain was troubled. *Would Ana be the same after having been a prisoner as long as she had been? It stood to reason that she'd been used by her captors. Would*

a violated woman feel she could take up where she had left off with a man who loved her? Would she be ashamed for him? Would love overcome all the negative doubts? Would she be with child? The thought suddenly jumped into Cooper's head. *Would she expect Jonah to feel the same if she carried or had another's man child?* So many questions and troubling thoughts? *Did they cross Jonah's mind also… they had to.*

"Damme… just bloody damme," Cooper swore. Had someone taken his wife, Sophia, it wouldn't have mattered… not one bit. It was Sophia who had shown Cooper the true meaning of love. After Sophia was killed, it was Maddy. Maddy, whose father was a British admiral. No, if someone took or had taken either of his loves, he'd seek the captors out. And no matter, if they had been used or not, he'd still love them… regardless he'd love them. Jonah would feel the same way. God help the blackhearts who took Ana. Cooper had no doubts their sorry arses would belong to Jonah and Moses. A shiver came over him as he thought, *I'd not want to cross those two.* He then remembered what John Will back in Savannah had said, 'Good men, good family, but they live by the feud. Not a family to wrong.' Well, they'd been wronged, and somebody was going to find out what it meant to wrong a man who lived by the feud.

A CHART OF THE GULF of Mexico lay open on Cooper's table. Another smaller map lay atop it at the upper corner. Johannes had a set of calipers in his hand and used them to point with.

"This is the Bay Saint Louis. Up here, this smaller chart is Lake Borgne." Emphasizing with the calipers, Johannes continued, "We can pass through here, and enter into the lake. The Pearle River flows into the lake here. A small settlement, Pearlington, lies just to the north. You have a choice, Jonah. You can pick up a couple of boats, or maybe Indian canoes, and travel up the Pearle to Jackson, or follow the river overland. I don't know about the overland route but if you choose the river, you'll pull against the current the entire trip."

"Aye, you'll be in no shape to fight if you do that," Mac threw in.

Donnie Hall volunteered, "I'm for the overland route but keeping an eye to the river."

Jonah asked, "Tired of the sea, are you?"

"Well, there's that but I's got a contacts at places along the river," Donnie replied.

"Then it's settled," Moses said.

"Praise the Almighty," Scrap mumbled. He'd not deny it, he was ready to plant his feet of firm soil again.

※

Waving good-bye to Cooper and the crew of the *Seafire*, the men picked up their packs and headed toward Pearlington. They'd not gone twenty steps when a thud and a curse were snorted.

"Confound it," Scrap swore. "It's not bad enough that the ship felt it was its duty to make me bust my arse but now the land is doing it too."

Laughing, Moses helped the little man up. Donnie took the man's pack and split it between him and his son, Tim.

Moses looked at Scrap and said, "It took a while to get your sea legs now you have to get your land legs back."

"I'll keep 'em when I get 'em back too," Scrap snarled. "Ain't fittin' for a man to cross more water than he can swim."

"Can you swim?" Tim asked, a devilish grin on his face.

"Ain't the point," Scrap replied.

Donnie hacked down a small sapling and trimmed the little branches off of it. "Here's a staff, Scrap. It ought to help you keep your feet on the ground and not yore bottom."

"Well, thank ye, Donnie. It's a real Christian, you are."

Pearlington was a small community named for the fishery, which took its name from the Pearle River. While it was not much of a town, it had a cemetery with headstones filled with French names from the previous century. A large building that served as a tavern and general store also had rooms to let at the top of the stairs.

The five men filled a rough hewn table by the window. It was not cold but it was cool. Had the smell of fish not been so great, the group would have chosen a table closer to the fireplace. A woman came over to wait on them. She wore an apron that was blood-stained and had fish scales on it.

"What'll ye be having?" the woman asked in an unfriendly voice. Her face looked tired and she pushed her graying hair back, showing dirty hands.

Jonah had suddenly lost his appetite, but Scrap didn't seem to pay any heed. "Is that catfish stew I smell on the fire?" he asked.

The woman said it was. "Catfish and crawdads."

"I'll take that and a tankard. You got any bread?" Scrap inquired.

"I'll see," the woman replied. Hearing Scrap's accent, she figured him to be a Mississippian and her demeanor improved. "Don't bother me none," the woman said, but pointing to Moses, she continued, "Homer might not like 'im eating inside. Mostly Negroes eat outside in the back."

"Well, Homer will just have to make an exception," Jonah declared firmly. "My brother eats where he pleases, not where he is told."

"No skin off my hide," the woman answered Jonah. "Only, I ain't Homer."

The bowls of stew and tankards of local beer were brought out along with a plate of thick golden brown cornbread. The stew was good, and the bread was not bad, but the only saving grace about the beer was that it was wet.

After eating, Scrap wiped his hands on his buckskins and slid off the bench. "Blast it to hell," he cursed. Reaching behind him, he pulled a splinter out. "Hope that got it all. I don't need any fester."

"I do too," Donnie said. "I don't know a soul who could stand to look at yore bottom side."

Scrap scowled but didn't reply. "I'll go see if theys any horse critters or mules about for sale. Reckon how many we'll need?"

Jonah replied, "Eight at least. Six horses and two mules. No, make that seven horses and two mules. Ana will need a horse." Nobody said anything, they just looked at Jonah.

"Try for nine critters with packs and saddles," Donnie said. "I don't like the thought of forking no animal without a saddle."

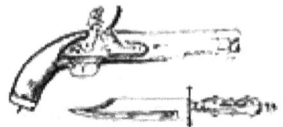

CHAPTER THREE

SCRAP FOUND SOME HORSES; they were not the quality of the Lee's stock, but neither were they nags. The mules were prime quality. One was a chocolate colored animal with a lighter, cream colored mane and tail, and was a particularly good buy. He was different than most mules in that he seemed to like human companionship.

"Somebody's pet, that 'un was," Donnie declared.

"I'll take him home if I can find a way," Jonah said. "I wonder how he'll ride."

"Not as good as a horse," Tim replied.

"Well, let's see." Standing perfectly still, the mule, who Moses dubbed Coco, let the saddle be placed on his back. Jonah then climbed on, only to find himself flat of his back.

"Throwed ya...ha ha!" Scrap was laughing and the rest were smiling.

"Reckon we know why he was sold," Moses volunteered. It took two more tries but finally Coco settled down.

"Thought you were going to get your head busted thar for a bit," Scrap joked. "You bout as stubborn as that thar mule."

"I just had to show the critter who's the boss," Jonah replied. "If he wouldn't carry me, he would not be much good as a pack animal, I'm guessing."

"Well, yer noggin' is still on yer shoulders, so I'm bettin' you've won... fer now."

THE GROUP HEADED OUT in a northerly direction, following the river. "Plenty of game hereabouts,"

Donnie mentioned as the group rode on.

Taking an interest in the river, Moses spoke. "Not too different from the rivers near home."

"Most of the rivers I've seen, those from Kentucky south at least, seem to share similarities," Tim volunteered. He'd not been much of a talker, so Jonah listened as he spoke. "Most look at the Pearle as a boundary between Mississippi and Louisiana," Tim continued. "There's these large areas of hardwood bottoms that's filled with game and were it cleared, the bottom land would grow good crops. Probably will be one day. Of course, there's big cypress swamps as you'd expect. Also like you'd figure, there are nasty critters as well… gators, cottonmouths, copperheads, and such. Black bears too. I've seen plenty of them. Hope I can get a crack at one of those bears."

"I love bear steak," Scrap said. "A little on the greasy side, but once you get the taste, nothing else satisfies."

"Not me," Donnie responded. "I'll take venison anyday. Give me a fat doe and I'll cook a backstrap fittin' for a king."

Tim didn't say anything but the look he gave didn't say much for his daddy's cooking. The group traveled at a steady pace, and about thirty minutes later they could hear the sounds of a village ahead.

"Logtown," Scrap said. "Used to be called Cabanage Latanier when the Frenchies had it. Of course, that was some years ago, after the war."

Jonah accepted by the war, he meant America's War of Independence. There wasn't much to the village. A sawmill seemed to be the center of activity. Stacks of logs were around the mill. A pile of clapboards were off to one side. The locals had taken advantage of the free clapboards. They'd built shacks, corn cribs, outhouses, and corrals, as well as pig pens out of the boards. Off to the side, a larger, better built structure sat. It was a tavern built out of logs. Care had been put into the construction. The logs were eight inch squared logs with dovetails. Shutters were open and the smell of meat on the spit was a natural draw.

"That smell has got my stomach growling," Moses stated.

"Your stomach is always growling," Jonah replied, but he was the first to turn his mount toward the tavern.

Entering the tavern, Jonah could see it was no different than a hundred others he and Moses had been in, other than the quality of construction of the building and the furnishings. Whoever built the fireplace and chimney knew his business as a stone mason. Chandeliers made from deer antlers hung from overhead beams. The coal oil lanterns that hung from the beams were not lit at this time of day. The shutters on the windows were open as were the front and back doors, letting in enough light so that the lanterns were not needed.

Without asking, a young girl, about ten to twelve years of age, filled wooden mugs with ale and brought them over to the men. "You be wanting to eat?" she asked, more a question than a comment.

"Yes," Donnie said, speaking for the group. The girl immediately turned and walked toward the kitchen.

"I guess we eat what's being fixed or do without," Moses thought aloud.

"This ain't the River Inn in Savannah with a four page menu," Jonah responded.

The men ate the food brought to them and then sat back. Donnie pulled out the stub of a cigar and relit it. Scrap bit off a chew from a tobacco twist. Deciding to join in, Jonah and Moses lit their pipes.

Looking at Tim, Moses asked, "You don't enjoy tobacco?"

"No, I never felt the urge to try it."

Outside the sound of horses could be heard. As men dismounted their horses, one man's voice could be heard through the open windows, "Get that mule outta my way so that I can hitch up my horse."

As a man passed too close to the rear of Coco, he kicked, catching the man fully in the chest. The man fell back against the horse of the man who had spoken. The horse reared up and its rider toppled off backwards, cursing as he hit the ground with a plop.

"By Gawd, I'll kill that animal," he swore.

Hearing the commotion, Jonah, Moses, and the rest of the group ran toward the door. As the thrown rider pulled his pistol out, a metallic click was heard.

"I think not, friend."

"That mule is a hare-brained critter," the rider replied.

"I'll agree but I'll not see him shot. Now, if you'll put away your pistol, I'll stand you men around."

"Like hell," the man swore again.

As he stood, Jonah could see he was a large man. One who used his size to make people cower down and to get his own way. His hair was sparse and he wore a scraggly beard to hide a pockmarked face. His teeth were yellow and stained with decay.

Seeing the man, Scrap recognized him as a flatboat man. "Part of the group yer looking for," he whispered.

Hearing this, Jonah stepped out of the door. "Let's talk," he said. He put his pistol down and stepped forward knowing the man was covered by Moses and his friends.

The man put his gun in his belt and as he stood he growled, "I talk best with my fist." He rose like a cat and slammed a big fist that caught Jonah behind his ear.

Jonah fell into the hitching rail dazed, and his eyes blurred. He'd not expected the big man's actions. Before he could recover, another man, the one Coco had kicked, landed a blow to his kidney that drove him to the ground. While down of the ground, someone kicked him hard, and a wicked state of pain lanced through his ribs.

Moses hit the man who had kicked Jonah in the face with the end of his rifle barrel. Blood spouted from busted lips, and broken teeth flew out of his mouth. Blood also poured from his nose. As the man fell, Moses clubbed him with the rifle butt, knocking him unconscious. At that time, a man jumped on Moses' back while another man yanked at his rifle. Tim kicked the man in the knee with such force the bone broke creating a loud sickening sound.

Meanwhile, Donnie came between Jonah and the pockmarked rogue with a wicked stab of his rifle butt to the man's gut. This doubled his foe over, but there was no quit in this man. As he fell, he snatched Donnie's feet out from under him. As Donnie fell hard on the ground, the rogue drew a long knife from a scabbard. When his hand rose to stab Donnie, a shot rang out. Blood gushed from a hole just at the top of the big man's nose. A surprised look came over the man's face a second before his eyes went blank and he fell backwards dead. The melee halted. One of the men stared at Scrap, who stood in the doorway. Smoke trailed from the end of his spent weapon. Men drifted apart as the fight was over. The men who were hurt were helped onto their horses, and then the rest of the men climbed on theirs.

As their opponents mounted up, one turned in his saddle. "You kilt Big Jim's brother, Scrap. Don't reckon that'll settle well. Guess you'd do well to get out of the country before we tell him."

Jonah had risen slowly. "You tell Big Jim that we are coming and hell is coming with us."

"We don't scare easy. You come," the rider snorted. "We can send hell yer way just as easily as you can bring it." With that said, the men rode away, leaving the dead man on the ground.

"He doesn't seem to scare any," Moses said.

"Naw, he doesn't," Scrap replied. "We's in his neck of the woods, so the odds are in his favor."

Jonah got slowly and painfully to his feet. The tavern girl stood at the door. "I'll fetch the blacksmith," she said. "He's the closest thing we got for a doctor. He does a good job on people and the animals," she mumbled as she walked off.

Several men, who had watched the fight, came over. "Not sorry to see this 'un gone," one of them said.

"Naw, me neither," his friend replied. "Not soon enough, howsoever."

"Kindly advice, friends," the man spoke to Jonah's group. "Were I you, I'd get shut of this place and head south. Big Jim will likely be in Picayune. By the time they reach him, you could have put a lot of miles between you. Bob was a bully and no account but he is… was Jim's brother, so I 'spect he'll be coming…and soon."

"Let him come," Jonah winced. "We weren't expecting trouble today but we'll be ready in the future."

Shaking his head, the man spoke to his friend, "Ready for an early grave, I'm thinking."

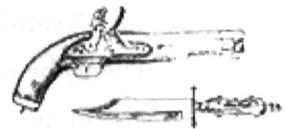

CHAPTER FOUR

WITH HIS RIBS BOUND tightly, Jonah and the rest of the group mounted their horses and mules and headed north. Hopefully, toward Ana, but definitely toward trouble. Mercifully, Coco didn't act up when mounted. Maybe he realized his rider was hurt and took pity on him. It was a grim looking group that went past Possum Walk. A small community of black workers was passed. Children stood in doorways and looked at the group of heavily armed riders. One child stepped outside and waved. A mother dashed outside and swooped the child up and ran back inside.

"Free darkies," Scrap said. "Most work at the Weston Mill or fish Bogue Homa. That's Choctaw for Red Bayou," he added. Riding a few more miles, he pulled up. "That's Devil Swamp over that away," he said, pointing with the barrel of his long rifle. "Hear tell a bunch of Choctaws and Creeks are hid out there. Staying away from Jackson's army, I'd say. Course, I hear there are runaway slaves and some white outlaws that found regular towns too hot for them there as well. Best we ride on. I ain't hankerin' for any brush wid a bunch of savages, regardless of color." The group agreed and pushed on.

The sun was going down and lights could be seen up ahead. "That'll be Napoleon," Scrap advised. "They say it was named for Bonaparte."

A store and a tavern sat between two large oak trees on one side and a huge cedar tree on the other side. The village sat on a bluff overlooking the Pearle. A small island sat in the river choked full of cypress trees. The store didn't have any rooms to rent but the owner offered the barn. "It'll keep the wind and rain off, and the cats keep the rats down." The group accepted and after supper turned in. The fight and ride had taken away a good deal of their stamina.

"Better keep a watch going," Jonah recommended.

"Yep, I ain't no trusting soul," Scrap admitted. Sleeping under a stoop would knock off the rain and wind but not the cold. It was open to the corral where the animals walked about freely, except Coco.

The mule would walk the perimeter of the corral but always came back and stood close to where the men slept. Jonah took the first watch even though the group said he should rest. He'd bought a bag of sugar at the store and when the mule walked up Jonah put a little clump in his hand and fed it to the mule. Coco's ears went back as he approached Jonah's outstretched hand.

"You bite me and I'll shoot you myself," he snarled at the beast. Almost like he understood, Coco stretched his neck out and curled up his top lip, showing a perfect row of teeth. He shook his head from side to side and then blew. Finishing his little act, the mule took the sugar and trotted off a ways.

Moses, his back against the wall, watched the event. *Damned, if he don't act like a hound*, he thought.

UP THE NEXT MORNING, the men were eating breakfast when a lone rider pulled up. Donnie saw and recognized the man at once. Looking around the room, the man was letting his eyes get used to the change in light. Donnie stood up at their table. Picking up the movement, the man turned and recognized Donnie.

Walking over, he waited until room was made on the bench and then sat down. Sitting down, he still towered over the rest of the group. Scrap barely came to his shoulders.

"Richard Smith," Donnie said by way of introduction. "He's a friend of yore friend." Jonah and Moses were then introduced.

Without any small talk, Smith reported his news. "The men with three closely watched women are in Picayune. They are reportedly headed south. Last night in Gainesville, I met up with a group you… ah, came in contact with a day or so back. 'Pears they have made better time than you."

"Not by much," Donnie said.

Whether he heard or not, Smith continued, "It didn't take much of the kill devil for them to start talking of a killing that was going to take place when they caught up with Big Jim and told him about Bob's death. Big Jim is the head of the trappers who keeps his women close."

"What now?" Donnie asked.

"My recommendation," Smith said, "is to head to Gainesville. It's not that far up the road. I'd wait there and put out the word the women are captives. They're not likely to help but they won't hinder either if the word is out. Big Jim's a tough man but his brother, Bob, has bullied and run roughshod over everybody until they're tired of it. You could likely ambush the group and as long it was out of town, not much would get said."

After finishing their meal and one more cup of scalding black chicory coffee, they moved on. Packing up, Jonah took his time and then when he could prolong it no longer, he climbed onto Coco's saddle. Expecting a repeat of yesterday, Jonah was relieved when it didn't happen. Not to say Coco took it freely. The mule arched its back and gave a few hops and then settled down.

"You ornery cuss, you did that just to make my ribs hurt…more," Jonah said.

No one laughed, even though they wanted to, but sore ribs were nothing to laugh at. It didn't take long to reach Gainesville, as it was only about three miles north of Napoleon. Like some of the other communities, it sat on a bluff.

"What's that?" Moss asked, pointing to a large floating building.

"That's a floating bar room and brothel. It floats up and down the river plying its trade. If things get to hot, they just up anchor and move, up, down, or across the river. Ingenious, is it not?" Smith said.

The woods had thinned out and Gainesville already had established farms with cut fields and cows were grazing about. Large barns were visible from the road and a church had been built. There was a timber mill, stores, and a hardware shop. A few fruit trees were seen, fig, peach, orange, and lemon.

The group pulled up at the store and bought a few things they didn't really need and stated the purpose of their trip. Jonah didn't hold back on how they'd been jumped back down the trail.

They repeated this at the tavern. Big Jim's men, having spent the previous night there, had already turned the town's sympathy towards Jonah's group. However, nobody wanted a gun battle in their town. Feeling that they'd done all they could do to sway the locals' opinions, the men headed out toward Picayune.

The decision was to come up on the group in camp, failing that, a good spot in the road that they could set up an ambush.

"These villages are so close together that they ain't likely to camp overnight," Donnie said. "They may stop to eat and rest about noon-time but that'd be it."

Tim rode ahead to keep his eyes out for Big Jim's group. He'd not ridden far when he turned and headed back. "There's a sharp bend up ahead, deadfalls all about and a few scattered rocks. It'd be a good place to set up. I'll ride on a few miles and see what I can see."

The bend in the road was a perfect place. Moses threw a rope across a deadfall to snake it into a better position.

"Hold up thar, Moses. You done hung up a big rattler," Scrap said.

Letting the snake crawl loose from the dead tree branches, Scrap stood back. "It's a good thang I saw him before he saw me. Otherwise, I'd have had to break the silence."

"You'd shoot him when you got a tomahawk in your belt?" Moses asked.

"No sir, I'd likely have screamed. I can't stand a snake, not any kind. Had one crawl across my legs once, thought I was dead. My heart jumped in my throat and I broke out in a sweat. The blasted thing seemed to enjoy my misery. It took its own sweet time crawling off. Packed up I did and then I rode several miles down the trail before I stopped."

"Why?" Moses asked.

"Well, son, he'd done claimed that spot. I couldn't rest thinking he might still be about."

"There could have been another one down the road," Moses responded.

"Coulda been but weren't," Scrap replied.

"Horse coming," Donnie said.

The men backed out of sight. The horse slowed as it got to the bend in the road. Tim walked around the bend and then stopped. When Jonah stepped out, Tim spoke, "There's a hill about two miles up. I went up the hill and looked about. They're coming, not more than a couple of miles back."

Moses had just snaked another deadfall into position. This one was in place across the trail, making it almost impassable as well as offering some protection from gunfire should it come to that. Soon the sounds of horses and the jangle of trace chains on a wagon could be heard.

As the lead rider rounded the bend, he cursed, "Whoa… whoa you damn nag."

The sound of others pulling back on the reins could be heard then. The driver of the wagon was not as quick. He hollered whoa and pulled back on the reins and stomped the wagon brake with his foot but too late. The wagon mules ran up into the horses, knocking one down. Had this not been serious business, Jonah would have laughed.

"Who, in all of creation, taught you to drive that wagon, Virgil?"

"Who told you to stop sudden like in a bend, Cleatus?"

Cleatus was the man whose horse was knocked to the ground. But the man Jonah had his eyes on had to be Big Jim. The man looked as big as the horse he rode. He had an unshaven black beard that was starting to be speckled with gray. A sweat-stained hat had fallen to the ground, revealing a bald top, but longish, dark hair that was over his ears and the collar of his shirt. His hands were huge; his skin had a leather brown appearance, and his face had a small mouth and close-set dark, almost black eyes.

Jonah had a primed pistol in his belt, a ready long rifle in his arms and another leaning against the deadfall.

Big Jim had just rearranged himself in the saddle when he noticed Jonah. "This yer idea of a joke?"

"No joke," Jonah replied. "Only way I could think of to parley."

"Parley. Hell we can parley over a jug or around a fire. This don't stand to be no simple parley."

While Jonah talked to Big Jim, Moses had moved to get a better view of the women in the wagon. They had fallen out when the wagon stopped suddenly and were just now righting themselves. One was obviously a squaw, and the next one looked like a mix breed. But the third… she could be Ana. Her face was worn and tired. Her hair was snarled and tangled, but… she was Ana. As he recognized Ana, she recognized Moses. She shook her head no, causing the other women to look. They looked but didn't make a sound. Moses put his fingers to his lips giving the 'shh' sign. But Ana was saying no with her head.

Back up front, Big Jim asked, "What is it you want to parley about, boy? I got a man to kill and women to sell."

"A year or so back, I lost a woman to an Indian raid," Jonah replied.

"Where was this?" Big Jim asked.

"Little village called Sandwich in the Northwest. We ran down the Red Devils that took her and found out a group of men, trappers and such, had saved her." Jonah thought saved sounded better than captured or taken prisoner. "We've been on the trail since."

"Well, if I did save such a woman and I still had her, I expect it'd take a right smart to pay for upkeep," Big Jim said.

You bastard, you've likely worked her senseless and now you want payment...ransom, Jonah thought. "I'm not a rich man, but I think it only fair that a man be paid for his troubles," he said. "What do you think it'd be, fair payment, I mean?"

This would tell. Big Jim chewed on a quid and looked about. If he knew there were four other rifles pointing at him, he didn't show any concern. "Reckon, close as I can figure, is three dollars a day. That amount times a year, that'll bring...shucks, let's just round it off and say a thousand dollars."

If Jonah had thought that would have sealed the bargain, he would have agreed. But something in the man's facial expressions, in the way he said a thousand dollars, and his snarling grin, let Jonah know there'd be a fight.

At that time, the man who had been present at the fight with Bob hissed, "That's one of 'em what killed Bob."

Big Jim was slick; he turned as if to speak to his rider. In doing so, his hand went to the pistol in his belt. He whirled around and fired. Jonah had already taken a step to his right. Big Jim's ball hit nothing but air. The big man was quick though. Realizing that he'd missed, he dropped the spent pistol and pulled another one from his belt and fired it while the smoke still lingered from the first shot. Spooking his horse with the pistol shot, Big Jim's horse reared and danced about. Jonah's first shot caught his foe in the shoulder, toppling him off of his frightened horse. All around gunfire broke out. Scrap drew bead on Bob's friend and hit him in the chest. Cleatus was trying to hide behind his horse with it dancing about. First Donnie and then Tim tried to get a shot but were unable to. Virgil grabbed a pistol and turned it back on the girls. Moses was shooting at a stationary target; his ball slammed into Virgil, knocking him down from the wagon. Crimson spread across his grease stained shirt.

Big Jim was still fighting, with the horses milling about, he reached down and took two pistols from Bob's dead friend. He trained his weapon on Jonah and shot through the branches on the deadfall. The ball hit a branch with a thud, but showered Jonah with dead bark. Some of the bark landed in his eyes and face. Seeing Jonah clearing his eyes, Big Jim jumped through the branches to get a clean shot. Jonah, trying to see past his watery eyes, caught a blur and fired. The ball hit Big Jim in the side, causing him to spin, but not go down.

Surrounded by Scrap, Donnie, and Tim, Cleatus threw down his weapon. Moses had made his way to the wagon where the three women had ducked down into the wagon bed. With a ball in the side and one in the shoulder, Big Jim leaned against the deadfall. Bleeding profusely from the two wounds, he tried to raise the rifle he'd picked up.

"Don't make me kill you," Jonah said.

Big Jim ignored the remark. Lifting the long rifle upward, he fired. Jonah must have fired an instant before Big Jim. Firing from the hip, he saw Big Jim's eyes widen. He heard the whoosh and felt the sting as a ball burned the top of his shoulder. Big Jim continued to stand, then his knees buckled and he sat on the ground. Not taking time to aim, Jonah's ball went high. Instead of hitting his man in the chest, he hit him in the throat. Blood poured from the wound. Big Jim made a gurgling sound and slumped forward dead.

"Whatever else he was," Donnie volunteered, "he was all man."

"Bury or swamp 'em?" Scrap asked.

"Swamp," Donnie and Tim answered at the same time.

Jonah laid his weapon down. Ana had to be in the wagon. Moses was to have sung out if she hadn't been. She was there, although she was not the beautifully washed and dressed woman he'd last seen. This woman was unwashed, unkempt, and worn out but he didn't care. It was Ana. Time, rest, and soap would take a lot of the physical abuse away. What about the mental abuse? They'd have to let time take care of that. Ana climbed down from the wagon as Jonah approached.

"No Jonah," she said.

"Shh."

"No, Jonah, I'm not the woman you knew."

Jonah paused for only a second. He reached out and pulled her to him. She resisted, but he held on.

Tears came down Ana's face, "You don't know what's happened to me."

"I know I've found you and will never let you go," Jonah replied.

"But..." her sentence was broke off. Jonah covered her mouth with his, again she resisted, but he wouldn't turn loose. She relaxed, although she didn't kiss him back, she didn't resist either.

THE BODIES WERE DUMPED into the swamp for the gators and other critters. The smell of blood mixed in the swamp water soon drew the animals in. With the one prisoner, they discussed whether to turn him loose or what. Finally Jonah called him over.

"Andy Jackson is in Mobile, and he needs soldiers. If you ride there and join his army, you can live. Otherwise, you join your friends in the swamp."

"Always did want to be a sojur. Can I take my guns?" the prisoner answered.

"You'll need them to fight the British," Jonah replied.

"Thank ye, sir. I'm headin' to see Andy."

Once he was down the trail, Donnie asked, "Think he'll join up?"

"Don't care, as long as he is gone," Jonah admitted.

"To Picayune or Gainesville?" Donnie asked.

"To Gainesville, I think," Jonah answered. "We know what's there."

"No telling about Picayune," Moses said, meaning Big Jim's men.

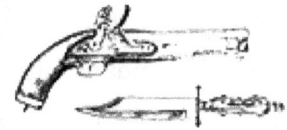

CHAPTER FIVE

Riding into Gainesville, Jonah's mind wondered. Ana was standoffish. Not the reunion that he had envisioned. But he'd not stopped to think of or imagine the abuse she'd likely been put through. Looking about, Gainesville was much like many other settlements. The main street would be baked by the summer sun, frozen hard as a rock in the winter and a quagmire of mud in the rainy season.

On the outskirts of the village were shabby, slab-constructed shacks, some with canvas roofs and dingy tents, lined the streets. At the center of town, the more permanent structures sat. The log tavern and inn, the general merchandise store were all constructed of planks. There was also a blacksmith's shop and stable. A hardware store specializing in river related needs. A grist mill and sawmill were also there. As the town grew, the restless men, the floaters, the brothel at the river's edge, and the scourge of mankind would disappear.

The decent, hard-working, respectable citizens would replace the drifters. The shacks and tents would disappear and be replaced by more businesses. The only thing that might last was the brothel. Wifeless men usually looked for three things to spend their wages on: drink, gambling, and women. Not necessarily in that order.

Pulling up at the tavern's door, the men dismounted and helped the women down. Richard Smith, his tall frame blocking the entrance, smiled, "Mission accomplished, I see."

Jonah nodded and entered the tavern, followed by Donnie and Moses along with the women. Scrap and Tim led the animals, including the two harnessed to the wagon, over to the blacksmith shop and stable. Inside the tavern, Jonah asked the owner how many rooms he had available.

"Got four," he advised. "Smith's occupying one, that means three are available. Ya'll seem friendly like, could be he'd share his room. There'd be an extra cost, of course."

"Of course," Jonah repeated. The women moved over next to the fireplace. "I'll take all three of your rooms," he said.

The tavern keeper nodded and then in a whispered voice, "We don't allow any sharing rooms between a man and woman less they be married." Jonah glared at the man, his stare making the man swallow hard. "No offense meant."

"None taken," Jonah replied. "I'll need tubs and hot water for the women. Do you have a girl who can help out with that?"

"Yes sir, I've got two. Mixed breeds they are but trustworthy."

"I'm not concerned about race," Jonah replied.

"Didn't figure you were traveling with the nig…" Jonah's glare cut the man off again.

When the tavern keeper didn't continue, Jonah said, "Hot baths for the women. Fresh clothes, undergarments if they're available. Dresses, if dresses are not to be had, britches and shirts will suffice. As well as shoes or boots and hairbrushes and mirrors. I reckon women set store by such things."

"I reckon they do. I've seen them carried at the store," the tavern keeper said. "Girls at the brothel fancy those things. You realize that this stuff will run you a pretty penny?"

Again, Jonah glared at the man. "I didn't expect it to be free." He pulled out his purse and counted out fifty dollars in coins. "We'll expect meals after the girls bathe and put on fresh clothes."

"Yes sir." The show of money had changed the man's attitude.

Moses walked in the door at that time. Seeing Jonah hand over the money he sidled up close. "Forgot to mention that we relieved those corpses of any valuables before dumping them into the swamp. Big

Jim had over two hundred in coin and the rest had about thirty dollars between them. We got the extra animals and wagon, as well."

"I think we'll need the wagon but we'll see about selling the horses," Jonah replied.

Moses looked at Jonah, "Something troubling you, brother?"

"I'm not sure if we should have dumped those men in the swamp."

"Humph," Moses snorted. "Gators and other critters got to eat, same as worms." This brought a smile to Jonah.

"So philosophically put," Jonah joked. At that moment, he and Moses gave way as the tavern girls toted steaming buckets of water upstairs.

CLEAN AND FRESHLY DRESSED, Ana and her two companions came down the stairs to the tavern's main room. Two tables were set up. Most of the men at one table while only Moses and Jonah sat at the other one. Ana looked much better, taking the space next to Jonah. The tavern girls had also picked up a bottle of lilac water and perfume. While not overpowering, the women had a clean, fresh smell that replaced the smell of wood smoke and body odor.

"Do you feel better?" Jonah asked.

"Yes," the three women said in unison. Ana's companions were smiling but Ana held her head down. After a moment of silence, she whispered, "We must talk."

Jonah placed his hand on top of Ana's and said, "We will."

Ana pulled her hand away quickly and tears fell from her eyes. "No, Jonah, don't touch me. I'm no longer fitting."

"Don't you think I should decide that?" Jonah asked.

"No! You don't understand, I'm not clean."

"You could have fooled me. You looked clean."

"That's not what I'm talking about." She leaned forward, "I've been used, Jonah, don't you understand? They took my body. They used me and when money was short, they sold my body. I've been used by countless men, over and over again. I hate myself. If I was not fearful of hell I would have killed myself. I hate my weakness. I'm... I'm not sure I would ever be able to stand a man touching me. Leave me, Jonah. Let me... let me just die."

"No, Ana, you've been through a lot. I know you hurt. But that's all behind you now. Give it time, Ana. You don't have to rush into any decision."

"You deserve more, Jonah."

"What I deserve, what I want is you," Jonah replied.

The food was brought, which ended the conversation. Ana's two friends tore into the food. It was plain that the fare was much better than they were used to. The two women paused and thanked Jonah.

"I'm Sally," the one girl said. She was the one that looked to be the mixed breed. "This is Fawn," she continued, introducing the youngest companion. "We haven't eaten like this since we was taken."

"They didn't feed you?" Moses asked.

"You might call it that. We fixed for the men and we eat what was left. Ana tried slipping out a piece of meat here and there, but she got caught and they beat her. I'm glad ya'll killed them, worthless shats that they were."

Moses' mouth dropped open at the girl's language, while Jonah just smiled. Ana couldn't help but smile at Moses also. "Sally is off the river. Bob killed her pa, and took her. She's more used to the ways of river folks than the genteel."

"What about Fawn?" Jonah asked.

"Almost the same story," Ana said, and then explained. "Her owner, she was sold to a man by a Creek Indian, who took her in a raid on a Cherokee village. The man who had bought her was playing cards but losing. He finally got what he believed was a winning hand. He couldn't make the pot so he put her up. When he was called, he had a full house. He got beat by four jacks. Trouble was he'd discarded a jack. His opponent, Big Jim's brother, had cheated. Fawn's owner called him on it, and took a ball in his gut for his troubles. He was still on the floor when Bob took Fawn and left."

"Right good people, your former companions," Smith volunteered.

The men had paused in their eating to listen to how the girls came to be with Big Jim, Bob, and their bunch. Soon the meal was over and one by one the men rose and drifted off. Sally and Fawn following their example rose and went to their rooms.

"You are not going to let me go, are you?" Ana asked, breaking the silence.

"No!"

"But Jonah…"

"Shh," Jonah said and put his hand on hers again. She didn't move it this time. "You are alive," Jonah said. "That's all that matters to me. The only thing in the past I care to think on is when we met. After that, the only thing that -mattered was finding you. Give it some time, a year, a month even. We find the first preacher; I'll make you my wife, then and there."

"I'll give it a few days," Ana replied. "That's all I can promise for now."

"That's enough," Jonah whispered. It was a starting place. He helped her up and they walked upstairs. Stopping at her room, Jonah leaned over and kissed Ana on the forehead, "Until tomorrow."

Once in the room, Sally spoke first, "That man, he's got it bad for you, child."

"I know, Sally, but it's not fair to him after I have been taken." Fawn, in her broken English, asked what she meant by 'taken'.

"You mean used," Sally said. "We all have, but they didn't take nothin you gonna miss. You got two legs and two arms. You got all of your parts. You ain't with child. Let me tell you something. You got back a chance to be a lady. What have we got? You ain't the first woman who's been used. You are alive, them girls at that whorehouse gets used every night. That don't keep another man from coming the next day and laying his money down. You reckon he cares what somebody else done took? No, cause he can't tell nothing is gone. Only us wimmin know that and those of us with good sense ain't telling." Fawn was smiling and nodding her head in agreement. "Was I you, I'd stop worrying about what has happened and think about what can happen. You think that man who came all this way here from Georgia, and killed the men what took us, and bought us all these clothes and such, is gonna worry about missing something he can't tell is gone. I been plain with you," Sally continued, "but somebody's gotta knock some sense into that head of yours. Was I you, I'd latch onto that boy and make sure he knowed how much I cared for him. He sure wouldn't have to worry about getting cold tonight. I'd warm his sheets for him."

Ana, now unable to hold back a smile at her vulgar mouth friend, said, "Maybe you're right."

"I know I'm right, and since we are friends, I'm not going to cut in. But if you don't change your ways, me and Fawn are gonna make sure we let them know how grateful we are."

"You little foul-mouth vixen, I believe you'd try to take my man," Ana said.

Sally looked at Fawn, "So now it's her man, is it?"

Surprised at her own words, Ana said, "Yes, he's my man. I just didn't want to hurt him."

"I 'spect the only way you'll do that is not to welcome him into your... your arms."

Ana hugged Sally and Fawn, "How could I have survived without you two?"

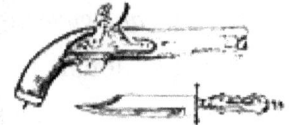

CHAPTER SIX

THE STAY OVER IN Gainesville lasted two more days. During those two days, Ana changed. Not totally, but Jonah was encouraged. The last night they went for a walk along the bluff, overlooking the Pearle River, and they had held hands. The moon had shone down and reflected off the lazy, slow moving river. Occasionally, a fish would jump. Otherwise it was mostly quiet. Holding hands seemed to Jonah to be the new beginning. Holding Ana's hand... hands that once were soft were now calloused and rough. *That would change*, Jonah promised himself. The lines in her face were relaxed and she'd laughed at one of Sally's remarks. Crude, though it was, that was Sally. Fawn didn't talk but always seem to be close to either Ana or Sally, her protectors. At supper the previous evening, Richard Smith spoke of Old Hickory. "I've enjoyed these last few days of leisure much as anybody, but now it's time for me to be heading down the trail. I got letters for Jackson that need to be gotten into his hands. I've got obligations and promises I've made, so I've got to be moving on." Moses noticed he didn't say notices to the president. "If it's agreed, we'll pull out at first light," Smith added.

The sun was a dim beacon to the east. The women had packed their dresses in a trunk and donned men's clothes. The wagon was packed and when Jonah turned to help Ana aboard he found her petting Coco, rubbing his nose and cooing to the ornery beast.

"Can I ride him?" Ana asked.

"You don't know this critter," Jonah responded. "He likes to start the day showing just how cussed he can be."

"Oh, he'll be alright," Ana said and kissed the mule on the nose.

Damn lucky mule, Jonah thought, *she ain't just come up and gave me a kiss yet.* Before he could protest, Ana stepped in front of Jonah and getting a foot in the stirrup, she climbed into the saddle. Coco just stood there.

"Yo' trouble," Donnie said, speaking to Jonah, "is you don't kiss the mule." This had everyone laughing, including Ana.

Scrap got on the wagon seat and warned, "Mind you rides to the right side, ma'am. I tends to spit to my left."

"I'll remember that," Ana responded, trying to remember a time when Scrap had not had a jaw full of quid.

It was late when the group stopped for the night. The men made camp, gathered firewood, and set up a tent of sorts while the women expertly went about cooking. It was a dry camp other than the water from the barrels attached to each side of the wagon. Soon the smell of coffee and frying bacon filled the air.

"That aroma has got my stomach to growling," Tim said.

"Beans, bacon, and frying pan bread, I've eaten a sight worse," Smith volunteered.

"It'd be worse now if Jonah was cooking," Moses joked. "We'd have burnt bread, scorched beans and the bacon would be questionable."

Everyone laughed, including Ana, but she ran a hand over his head as she passed him. They could laugh all they wanted. Just to feel Ana's touch made the world feel right.

The next morning, they greeted the sun. After reaching Bay Saint Louis, they followed the coast road east, through Pass Christian to Mississippi City and several nameless villages. Most of the villages depended on the abundant forest for lumber or the Gulf of Mexico for fish as a means to survive.

"Wonder how many of these places will be here in ten years?" Moses thought aloud.

A number of Indians were in most of the villages causing Jonah to wonder how long it would take before they were pushed out. Reading Jonah's thoughts, Moses said, "Amazing how well people get along until the white man's greed takes a hold."

Smith heard the comments, but didn't say anything. He was still trying to figure out the bond between Jonah and Moses. It was a long, deeply seated bond, that much was obvious. But it was none of his business. Scrap, Donnie, and Tim seemed at ease with it. The girls, especially Ana, understood. If it came up, he'd find out the answers to his questions, but he'd not bring it up. No sir, not Richard Smith... his mama didn't raise no fool.

The group had been traveling steady for a week when they rode into the village of Biloxi, Mississippi. Like the other town that had makeshift shacks, Biloxi also had a few larger more permanent dwellings. The village had a tavern with rooms, a general store, a large blacksmith shop, and a livery stable. A fishing village could be seen in the distance. People milled about in various dress, from store bought to homemade clothes, linsey woolsey to buckskins. A few Indians were mixed in the lot.

"I'll go check on some rooms," Jonah volunteered. "Donnie, if you will bring the girls' trunk."

"I'll head to the stable with Moses," Scrap said.

Smiling, Smith said, "I'll head to the tavern, and see if I can catch up on any local news."

A LARGE TABLE WAS SET up for supper. The serving girl looked at Moses suspiciously but didn't say anything. Roasted pork, greens, buttered hominy, fresh baked bread, and a blueberry pie were served.

"Blueberries grow wild hereabouts," the proprietor of the tavern said. "I strung some rope and set out some cuttings and the next thing you know, we have enough so that my wife can put up jars of blueberries. They are good for pies and puddings and such. The wife even makes sweet bread with them."

As the group was finishing their meal, the man from the livery rushed in. Spying the group, he shouted, "You got trouble. A man says he's gonna shoot yo' mule."

"Not again," Scrap swore.

Everyone jumped up, but Ana being the closest to the door, was up and racing toward the stable. Once outside, the slap of leather against flesh could be heard. Coco was jumping about and braying while a man with a plow line beat him. Without thinking, Ana charged into the man. Turning his focus from the mule to Ana he slapped her. The blow was such that it knocked her to the ground. The next sound was the eerie unmistakable sound of a hammer on a weapon being cocked.

Jonah hissed, "Mister, if you value your life as much as I value my woman, you'd best back off."

"She attacked me," the man said. "I didn't know that she was a woman."

"You were beating my mule," Ana shouted.

In the middle of all this, Jonah had to smile, *my mule is it*. Well, it could be her mule as far as he was concerned. "If you apologize to the lady, you can go on about your business," Jonah offered.

"I ain't apologizing fer nothing," the man replied.

Jonah had already started to think of him as flop hat. The brim to his hat was broken so it just flopped over. He wore a dirty shirt with missing buttons. His pants were tucked into worn boots and were held up with suspenders. He was as wide as he was tall. He looked as if he hadn't shaved in a week and smelled as if he hadn't bathed since the last rain.

Jonah took a step forward and helped Ana up. "If you want to live, stranger, you got ten seconds to apologize. Start counting, Moses."

"Ten, nine, eight."

"You are mighty big with your entire backup. Were it just the two of us, I'd show you who would apologize."

"Five, four, three," Moses continued counting.

"No, Jonah, don't kill him," Ana pleaded.

Jonah held up his hand and Moses stopped counting. He handed the rifle in his hand and the pistol in his belt to Donnie. "You can have your chance," he said. "Nobody will interfere, but just for the record, why were you beating my… my woman's mule?"

The livery stable man spoke up, "He tried to get the mule to open his mouth to look at his teeth. Said that he might take him. When the mule wouldn't open up, he grabbed the animal's upper and lower lip and went to twisting. The mule jerked his head back making the 'idjet' lose his grip." Now laughing, the man continued, "That mule laid its ears back and chomped down on his tormentor. That's how it started."

"I'm going to kill that mule and then you, Jude. You'll learn to keep your trap shut."

"Bold talk for a fat man," Jonah responded.

"You'll see," Flop said and charged Jonah. He was quick… real quick.

As he rushed, Jonah threw a punch with all that he had. It split Flop Hat's ear, knocking him to the ground. But he was up quickly. *Oh no!* Jonah thought. Angered, the man rushed in. Jonah had given him his best shot but it didn't appear to faze the man. It certainly didn't slow him down. Flop Hat rushed again, but just before he got there he dove at Jonah's legs. A terrible pain went through his knees as he fell. *Are they broke*, he wondered.

Flop Hat crawled upward toward Jonah's chest. His weight squeezed the air out of Jonah. As he scrambled forward, Jonah slapped the man's ears on each side with cupped hands. This had the desired effect. Flop Hat's hands went to his ringing ears. As he did, Jonah aimed a blow for Flop Hat's chin. The man pulled back as he saw the blow coming… he shouldn't have. Instead of on the chin, the blow caught him in the throat. As he fell over, gasping for air, Jonah arched his back and bucked. Off his balance, Flop Hat rolled over, still gasping for air.

Jonah got to his feet only to find his adversary facing him. *Damn, there's no give*, Jonah thought, just as a roundhouse punch caught him, sending him backwards into his friends... that's what saved him.

Flop Hat, waiting for the crowd to back away, was now surprised when Jonah got up. "Well, you got more than most," he said. "It's a pleasure to whoop a real man." With that, Flop Hat rushed again, only this time Jonah was ready. When Flop Hat dove, Jonah kicked out snapping the man's head sideways. Yet like a cat, Flop was back on his feet and rushing again. He hit Jonah a glancing blow that dazed him. He'd just barely cleared his head when Flop Hat was on him again. Arms and fists were flying like a windmill. A right grazed Jonah's cheek just below the eye and it swelled immediately, making it difficult to see. The next blow busted his lips. Shaking his head, Jonah was just able to sidestep the next rush. He landed a blow to Flop Hat's gut, doubling the man over.

"That's it," Tim and Smith sang out in unison.

With Flop Hat bent over, Jonah gave him a wicked blow to the kidney. Flop raised a tad and a hand went to his side. Jonah then swung with all he had left, hitting Flop Hat in the chest, over the heart. Flop Hat fell backwards in the dirt, out cold. Suddenly there were whoops and hollers; some even gave a shrill whistle.

"What a fight," the tavern keeper swore.

Amid the backslaps, the handshakes, and the shouting of accolades, Jonah and his group made it back to the tavern. After a quick glass of corn squeezing, Jonah was helped upstairs.

"Put him in here," Ana ordered. "Now go get a bucket of warm water."

When the water and a clean cloth were brought up, Sally turned to the men. "Out, out all you sidewinders. Let Ana take care of her man."

They backed out and as Sally left, she looked at Ana, "You got you a man, darling. Now take care of him."

Ana helped Jonah out of his dusty, torn shirt. She carefully washed his wounds, and kissed his busted lips gently. She then went over and latched the door. Taking Jonah's boots and britches off, she leaned over and kissed him again. She then stood upright and unfastened the buttons on her dress, letting it slide to the floor. Her undergarments came next. Watching through swollen eyes, Jonah marveled at her beauty. She'd lost weight, but otherwise this was the woman he loved.

"To the victor goes the spoils," Ana said softly, leaning over she blew out the lantern and climbed into the bed with Jonah.

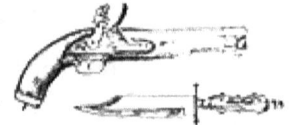

CHAPTER SEVEN

The next morning the animals were either saddled or hitched to the wagon and ready to go as Jonah, stiff and sore, made his way downstairs to eat. His lips were bruised and swollen, making it hard to eat and he had to wait until the coffee was nearly cold to sip it. But, while his physical aches and pains were evident, he was a happy man... a sated man.

"The animals alright this morning?" Jonah asked.

"Yep, we was worried there might be trouble, so we set-up a watch, two hours at a time. Waste of time probably, but you never know."

"You should have called, I would have taken a turn," Jonah replied.

"Naw," Donnie answered for the group. "You did your job."

Sally leaned over so only Ana could hear and said, "Did he?" Ana's face flushed but she smiled. "Guess he did," Sally said in a whisper.

It was over four hours later when they stopped in Gautier. They watered the animals and let them rest. They'd come twenty miles since first light.

"We can layover here or push on," Scrap said. "It's another five miles to Pascagoula. After that, it's two days to Mobile."

They decided to push on to Pascagoula so, after an hour's rest, they continued on. They'd just made it to the settlement when the wagon's back axle broke. Putting the women on horseback and moving the supplies to the front of the wagon, they made it to the blacksmiths. Rooms were not available for everyone, so while the women enjoyed a bed and a bath, the men slept in the stables.

It was mid-morning before the axle was replaced. "Outta have an extra one," the blacksmith informed them. Of course, he did. The price was reasonable though so Jonah bought it and paid for the repair and livery bill.

"I won't charge you for sleeping here since you paid for everything else," the blacksmith said.

"Thank you," Jonah replied, but he had already decided that he wasn't going to pay for sleeping in the hay.

It took two and part of a third day to reach Mobile. The presence of Jackson's army was noted right off. As they found rooms at an inn, Smith commented, "I'd have thought Jackson would have had more soldiers than this."

"He does," the innkeeper said, hearing the comment. "He lit out for Pensacola two days ago to take the Spanish fort. Hear tell that he said he'd be back in a week."

"He must not think much of the fort's defense," Donnie said.

"Ole Andy doesn't think much of no Spaniard in general, from what I hear," the innkeeper answered.

"You seem well informed," Smith stated.

"Well not really, just talk mostly. I did hear that when he gets back he's headed to New Awleens. They got word that's where the Redcoats are going."

"New Orleans," Moses repeated. "We should have stayed at Bay Saint Louis."

"How'd we know?" Jonah responded.

"Are we going back to New Orleans?" Sally asked. "I thought we were going to Georgia."

Jonah didn't reply, he just looked at Ana who had a stunned look on her face.

LATER THAT NIGHT AFTER the evening meal, Jonah sat by Ana in two big rocking chairs. "It's my job," he said. "Much as it was when we first met. I've given my word to the president." Ana listened but didn't speak. Jonah sat forward in his chair, "You can stay with me in New Orleans. I'm sure that we can find some quarters; or Moses with Donnie and Tim can take you back to Georgia."

"No, we are not going to be separated again." Ana's eyes began to water and soon tears ran down her face. "I'm not leaving you again. Wherever you go, I'm going to. I just wish this damn war was over. I worry you may be wounded or killed. I'd kill myself if you were ever taken from me again."

Jonah stood up and pulled Ana up to him. "Shh," he whispered. "Nobody will ever separate us if I can help it." Leaning down, he kissed her forehead and then her lips. The salty taste from her tears burned his lips. "Do you want to get married here, tonight or tomorrow?"

Ana replied, "I thought you wanted us to get married in Georgia, at your home."

"We can get married anytime you desire. We can always have another ceremony or a celebration when we get home," Jonah said.

"Humph, you just want to take me to your bed," Ana answered him.

"True, but I've wanted that since I first laid eyes on you."

"You lecherous heathen."

"Guilty," Jonah said with a smile.

"No, we'll wait, unless I become with child," Ana responded.

"Deal," Jonah said, and hugged her to him.

"That was a might fast, I'd say."

"I want you so bad, I'd agree to most anything," Jonah replied.

"I bet you would, buster."

He didn't mention it, but Jonah had noticed Ana's vocabulary had changed. Something harder, her French accent and pronunciation were gone as well, probably lost during her captivity. One tends to speak and act like those they associate with Mama Lee had said when she'd heard Jonah curse. You lay with pigs, you'll act like pigs. Maybe going to New Orleans for a while was a good thing. Not that he cared.

But to be around ladies again might help Ana. If not, he still loved her, regardless of how she spoke.

"What ya'll doing out here in the dark?" Sally asked.

Now that's one that'd take some explaining were I to take her home, Jonah thought, unable to keep from smiling.

Jonah, Ana, and Richard Smith were sitting on the veranda of their inn when excitement filled the street.

"He's back, Old Hickory is back. Smote the Spaniards, he did."

"It won't be long now, my dear, when you get to meet our general," Jonah said, speaking to Ana.

They didn't have long to wait. The street was soon lined and crowded with people expecting to see the tall, lean, hawk-eyed Tennessean, who his admirers called Old Hickory. The inn steps were suddenly filled with people trying to get a better view. The proprietor pushed a few off the top step so he and his family could see the approaching column of soldiers. Richard towered over the onlookers below him, but Ana had trouble seeing so he and Jonah helped her up into a chair so she could see the hero of Horseshoe Bend.

As the crowd cheered, Jackson rode stoically down the street. While his head didn't turn, his eyes took in everything. He spoke suddenly to his aide, who pulled out of the column and rode over to the inn. People had to part and give way for the rider.

As the rider approached the porch, a smile broke out on his face, "Jonah, did you make it to Washington and back already?"

Smiling, Jonah stepped forward and shook his friend's hand. "Captain, I see you still have your hair." The man smiled, but Jonah could see his eyes were on Ana.

Jonah turned to Ana, "My dear, this ruffian in a soldier's uniform is Captain John Reid. He's General Jackson's aide."

"Captain Reid, this is my fiancé, Miss. Anastasia Greenville."

"Miss Greenville, a pleasure. How was Washington?" Captain Reid asked.

"Hot. They burned it to the ground," Jonah replied.

Captain Reid suddenly turned white. "I don't think the general knows. He's wondered why there has been no response to his dispatches."

"The government is in disarray, John."

Richard Smith stepped forward, "I have dispatches for the general. Some are from the governor, and some I believe have been forwarded from Washington."

Jonah knew when Smith said governor; it was taken for granted it was from the Tennessee governor. Had it been from any other governor, it would have been made known.

Captain Reid sat erect on his horse, "I must take my leave, Jonah, Madam." Looking back at Jonah, Reid spoke again, "The general's compliments, and would you care to dine this evening?" He hesitated and then added, "I'm sure the invitation is also extended to you as well, Madam. There may be a few minutes where the general would like to talk to Mr. Lee alone, but I can assure you, Madam, that I will be available and quite happy to escort you and see to your needs while Mr. Lee is occupied."

"Only too happy, I'd say," Jonah replied in mock jealously.

"Now, Jonah, I'm sure Captain Reid will be the perfect gentleman," Ana said, smiling.

"By all means, Madam," Reid replied with a smile in his voice.

"I'm not really worried, John. Moses will be about," Jonah said.

"I'm sure," Reid replied, making a show of swallowing hard. This caused the entire group to laugh.

As soon as Captain Reid rode off, Ana turned to Jonah, "I simply must find something to wear. I cannot dine in such attire."

"You folks go ahead," Smith volunteered. "I will deliver my dispatches to the general."

Jonah nodded, but his mind was on Ana. Her rehabilitation seemed to be progressing in leaps and bounds.

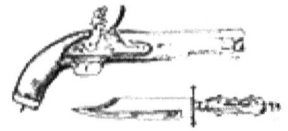

CHAPTER EIGHT

THE EVENING MEAL WAS plain but delicious. It consisted of corn in a buttery sauce, yams with cinnamon, green beans and roasted pork. Dessert was a simple bread pudding that had a cinnamon sugar glaze.

"The only wine we have is a local grape called the muscadine," Jackson said, apologizing. "It is a little sweet for my taste, but if you indeed intend to travel with Jonah, as I'm led to believe, the fare should improve rather quickly."

This caught Jonah's attention, and Jackson saw the interest on Jonah's face. Jackson liked Jonah, but still regarded him as the president's man. "We will march for New Orleans within the next few days," Jackson announced.

Glancing at Smith, Jonah saw no change in the man's face at the news. *He either already knew or was a good card player*, Jonah thought.

"We will speak of this later," Jackson continued. "Right now, let's enjoy our meal that has been graced by the addition of the lovely Miss Greenville. Remind me, dear, when Mr. Lee is not around, to tell you what a rogue you've saddled yourself with." After the expected chuckle, Jackson said, still smiling, "In truth, Miss Greenville, had I a son, I'd very much want him to be as Jonah. You see, in spite of my earlier comments, I am very fond of him." He then rose and lifted his glass, "A toast to the future Mr. and Mrs. Jonah Lee. I do expect an invitation to the wedding."

Smiling, Jonah rose after the toast had ended. "To General Jackson, the greatest leader America has known." After the toast,

Jonah thought, *I may have pushed that a bit, but I'm not sorry*. In his mind, the general had something he'd found little of in other commanders—audacity. Colonel Richard Mentor Johnson had it, but to the same degree? Jonah wasn't sure.

Jackson didn't dress the part. To look at his tall, lean frame, he looked like a man old before his time. He was constantly in pain from old wounds; he still carried a lead ball from an attempt on his life. With all this, one only had to look into his eyes. There one could see the man with the intestinal fortitude of steel. God help the man who stood in Jackson's way. But would he be enough to withstand the forces of the British Empire. If he had to bet, he'd bet on Andy by Gawd Jackson, Jonah realized.

THE TRIP TO NEW Orleans was a haze. Jonah thought he'd made good time in the trip across Mississippi to Mobile, but he realized it was nothing compared to the pace Jackson set. Thinking back to the relaxed meal, the last night of Ana and he having a peaceful night together was the night they dined with the general. After supper, when Ana was excused, Jackson brought Jonah up to date on his latest intelligence. This was after Jonah summarized the trip he and Moses had taken to Washington and the British attack.

"I have long believed that the British would attack Mobile and go overland to New Orleans," Jackson said. "I'm still not totally convinced this might not be the case. However, I've had several letters from Governor Claiborne, who is in a panic. He feels he now has proof positive that the British intend to attack New Orleans. He gathered this information from the pirate LaFitte. He furthermore has a letter from an acquaintance in Cuba stating that the British intentions include freeing the slaves."

Risking Jackson's anger, Jonah mentioned his knowledge of LaFitte. "General, before the war, I had the good fortune of becoming friends with Eli Taylor, a sea captain, and his protégé at that time, who now commands an American privateer. We traveled overland from Thunderbolt to New Orleans. There we met Jean LaFitte and some of his brothers. They, as you can guess, are not well thought of by Claiborne. Having said that, he is a man of impeccable dress, and a gentleman. He was readily accepted in all the circles in which we were invited. He has supplied the city with slaves, staples, and yes, luxuries at bargain prices. He holds a Letter of Marque. I agree, the letter is loosely adhered to. But I have it on the word of Captain Taylor and Captain Cooper Cain, the man has never attacked an American ship."

"So this ah… gentleman is a personal friend of yours, Jonah?"

"I'd not go that far, sir, but were it so, I'd not be ashamed." Recalling Barataria, Jonah added, "He has the wherewithal to defend New Orleans almost singlehandedly."

"My word, man, are you that taken with a pirate…a thief?" the general asked.

Jonah rose up, clearly insulted. General Coffee and the other officers were suddenly on edge. Clinching his fist and trying to gain control of himself before saying something he'd regret, Jonah hissed, "Thank you for the meal, sir." He turned to Coffee, "It was nice seeing you again." Looking back at Jackson, he said, "I must bid you good evening, sir."

As he turned to leave the room, Jackson called to him, "Wait."

Slowly, Jonah turned, "I truly must go, General. It would be for the best."

Jackson rose and walked the few steps to Jonah. Placing a hand on Jonah's shoulder, he said, "Please accept my apology, Jonah. You are a friend who has always given wise council. Even when you knew it to be contrary to my thoughts." Jonah shook the general's offered hand. "Now, gentlemen, seeing the lovely Miss Greenville reminds me that I am overdue in writing Rachel."

Over the next few days, Jonah had time to talk to Captain Reid and Captain Lieupo. They told of how Jackson had sent a dispatch to Washington, unaware of the troubles there, that he intended to attack Pensacola. They also told how Jackson had garrisoned the undermanned, under gunned Fort Bowyer, which guarded the mouth of Mobile Bay. On September 12th, the British then attacked as Jackson had predicted. However, the Americans were ready. The twelve-gun fort surprised the British. They not only beat off the attack but also sank a British frigate. Word quickly arrived that the British retreated to Pensacola, Florida.

Smiling, as was his like, Captain Lieupo told of the attack on Pensacola. "Now that Britain's war with France was over, Spain and Britain were no longer enemies. Pensacola was the second oldest city in Florida. It was normally a settlement of around one thousand residents. The Spanish governor had supported the Indians' attack on Fort Mims. Because of that and the defeat by Jackson at Horseshoe Bend, Pensacola suddenly became home to nearly another thousand wounded and starving Red Stick Indians. The city is defended by Fort San Miguel—which is located on the north end of Pensacola Bay. This fort also provides protection for the settlement. Another fort, Fort San Carlos de Barrancas, situated on Santa Rosa Island fronts the Gulf of Mexico. This fort provides the most strategic control and protection of the upper gulf. Hearing from scouts in August, 1814 that the British had established a presence there with the full cooperation of the Spanish governor, Don Mateo Gonzalez Manrique, angered Jackson. He worried that the British would use Pensacola as a base to attack the southern United States, so he requested permission to attack. He had gained evidence that Pensacola had two hundred Royal Marines under the command of Major Edward Nicolls. It was the same Major Nicolls, who was part of the unsuccessful attack on Mobile Bay. When no word came denying Jackson's request, he decided to rid the British from our American soil, even though it meant invading Spanish territory. After the arrival of General John Coffee with his volunteers, Jackson attacked. On the morning of November 7th, with two thousand mounted Tennessee volunteers, seven hundred regulars and a detachment of Mississippi territory dragoons, the attack began."

Captain Lieupo continued his narrative, "What Jackson did, was send five hundred soldiers in a feinting move to the west side of Pensacola. When they made an attack, Jackson, with the majority of his force, attacked Fort San Miguel on the east side. Unlike Horseshoe Bend, it was over before we knew it. The Spanish, a force of about five hundred men was quickly overrun. Hoping to keep Jackson from laying ruin to the city, the governor surrendered immediately. All of a sudden, he wasn't so high and mighty anymore. He sent Jackson all kinds of humble, flowery letters. Seeing that we took the fort and city, the British turned tail. They abandoned Fort San Carlos, sailing away on British warships that they had anchored on the coast."

Thinking militarily, Jonah asked, "What was the cost?"

"Light," Captain John Reid volunteered. "We lost seven, and ten or eleven were wounded, nothing too serious. We counted fifteen Spanish killed, and are not sure how many were wounded."

"A great success, wouldn't you say?" Lieupo asked.

"Yes, if we can hold it," Jonah replied.

"I think we will; the general left two regiments to garrison the city. I tell you, Jonah, you'd have been dismayed had you seen the ferocity of our men as they attacked."

"I don't reckon I've seen such before," Jonah replied.

"I reckon by now, that the word has gotten out. This will help us with volunteers, hopefully," Captain Reid added.

"For New Orleans, you mean," Jonah asked.

Reid nodded, "We've beaten them back at Mobile and Pensacola. The general now agrees that that is the most logical place for them to attack... so we march."

THE FORCED MARCH TO New Orleans left the entire army and those traveling with them bone tired. But not one person complained. If Jackson, worn down by dysentery, could push himself, the rest were inclined to keep up without complaint. Daily, riders rode in describing the wholesale panic. The governor, who was detested by most, could not bring the different factions together, so the city was defenseless. On top of one mistake after another, Claiborne allowed Commodore Daniel Patterson to attack the best potential ally the city had... Jean LaFitte, at Grand Terre. Rather than oppose Patterson, LaFitte ordered a retreat to nearby islands. Patterson captured eighty men, including Dominique York. It was later said that Patterson plundered Grand Terre's merchandise to the tune of half a million dollars, calling it spoils of war and never repaying a cent of it.

It was common knowledge that the dispatch rider informed Jackson that LaFitte, with more than two thousand men under his command and a vast number of warships, could have wiped out Patterson in a single blow. He didn't though, standing by his resolve to never fire on the American flag. "It be a mystery to me," the rider said, "with such stupid blunders by Claibo, why LaFitte didn't jine up with the Redcoats. He'd be richer and they'd have the city."

Jackson glanced at Jonah, who sat on his horse listening to the report. "It appears your conviction of the man bears considerable thought, Jonah."

"It also speaks tons when the governor is so despised, that he is openly criticized by the use of Claibo as his name," Reid said.

"You're right, Captain Reid. As you were, Jonah. I fear we have little time to reach the city."

After that day, the army traveled from sunup to sundown. The scout, Richard Smith, had become close friends with Jonah and Ana on the march. When he was not out scouting the trails, he took most of his meals at their camp, along with Captain Lieupo. Moses and

Scrap provided fresh meat while Donnie and Tim took turns driving the wagon and seeing to the needs of the animals. Donnie once volunteered to relieve either Scrap or Moses, and do some of the hunting. Tim quickly and jokingly said, "Naw, we'd better leave the arrangement as it is. You ever see Paw shoot, you'd know what I mean." Everyone laughed, but the arrangements continued as they were.

It was on the first of December that a less than impressive army arrived in the city of New Orleans. Many of the residents in New Orleans were alarmed at what they saw. The city's future depended on this wore out, scraggly-looking army. They looked at the appearance of the army and not the resolve of Andrew Jackson. They were soon to realize their mistake in making rush judgments.

PART II

We looked down the river and we seed the British come
There must have been a hundred of 'em beating on the drum
They stepped so high and they made the bugles ring
We stood behind our cotton bales and didn't say a thing.

We fired our guns and the British kept a coming
There wasn't nigh as many as there was awhile ago
We fired once more and they began to runnin'
On down the Mississippi to the Gulf of Mexico.

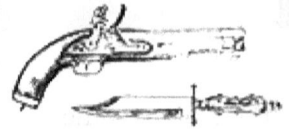

CHAPTER NINE

JONAH WATCHED JACKSON'S FEATURES as he rode through the streets of New Orleans. Even though he was not yet fully recovered from the fatigue of Horseshoe Bend, Mobile, and Pensacola, Jackson still cheerfully embraced the responsibility of defending a city that Richard Smith had confided that several felt was defenseless. The city had no forts, no navy to speak of, and nobody that had the ability to bring the different factions together. Could Andy Jackson? Unlike any other city in the United States, the language was so much different that just communicating would prove a chore. It was like they were in a city of strangers.

Riding just behind the general was Major Hughes, commander of Fort Saint John. Major Butler rode just to the left behind Major Hughes, and Captain Reid was to the right.

A well-dressed man ran up to the general and fell in beside his horse. "If you will be so kind as to follow me, General, the governor is waiting." Jackson gave the briefest of nods but followed the man.

The cavalcade came to a halt in front of a very elegant residence. Jonah wished Ana was up closer to the front so that she could see the splendor. It was said that the residence had belonged to Daniel Clark. He had been Louisiana's first representative to the United States Congress. A very powerful and influential man, he'd died soon after the war started. Here at this residence, Jackson was met by Governor W. C. C. Claiborne, several members of the Committee of Public Defense, Commodore Patterson, in his naval uniform, the mayor, Nicholas Girod, and Edward Livingston, the city's leading attorney and supporter of Jean LaFitte. Standing by Livingston was the District Attorney, John R. Grymes.

Jonah saw impatience building as Jackson sat through all the bureaucratic motions. Finally, Jackson replied to the welcome. His response was brief, "I have come to protect the city and drive the enemy into the sea, or perish in the effort." The applause was as expected.

Jackson then paused and appeared to stare into the souls of every man present. Jonah was not surprised when Jackson, in a diplomatic way, said that he expected the citizens of New Orleans to rally around him, to cease all differences and divisions, and unite with him to save the city. Not one person doubted that while the hawk-eyed general spoke diplomatically, he would tolerate no less than full cooperation. Jackson's speech was repeated to the French speaking by Mr. Livingston. Once Livingston had finished, the cheers, whistles and applause began anew.

A carriage was suddenly made available, probably by the governor, Jonah decided, and the entourage then proceeded to the general's new headquarters, 106 Royal Street. It was a new brick building. A flag soon flew from the third story, and without taking pause to rest; Jackson started planning the defense of the city. Many would have looked at the man, so worn down by bad health and fatigue, and wondered if he would be able to pull off the impossible.

After ten days on horseback, Jonah was wore out, everyone was. But not one had the will of Jackson. It was that will, Jonah knew, that would triumph in the end. While he had cause to disagree with Jackson's Indian policy, he knew the fate of New Orleans rested upon the stoop-shouldered Jackson.

HOTEL PROVINCIAL SAT BACK off the street under a group of giant old oak trees, where gray moss hung from their branches. It was as remembered from Jonah's trip to the city with Cooper Cain and his wife at the time, Sophia; Captain Eli Taylor and his wife Deborah, or as she preferred, Debbie.

Jonah watched Ana's reaction as they drew up to the hotel. Her eyes were wide open and her hand covered her mouth. "What a beautiful place. It's so… so romantic."

Smiling, Jonah hopped down and helped Ana from the wagon. Moses got off his horse and grabbed as many bags as he could take. Fawn and Sally grabbed the rest. As they neared the door, two black boys in hotel uniforms rushed out to take the bags from the women, leaving Moses to struggle with his. *Damn, from the rags on their backs when we rescued these wenches, they sure have collected a lot,* he thought.

A beautiful lady sat at a small table by a large bay window. She rose and approached the group. "It's M'sieur Lee, is it not?"

Smiling, Jonah responded, "Mademoiselle Renee, you remembered."

Mademoiselle Renee said, "Captain Cain was here a month or so back. He brought a letter from Captain and Mrs. Taylor to expect you. You are to have their suite. I am sorry to say that I only have one other room available. With all this talk of war, things are so… in chaos. We, of course, have quarters for the servants to stay in, if that's agreeable."

Jonah, not sure what Mademoiselle Renee meant, looked at Ana. "Nice, she means the quarters are nice," Ana said.

Jonah nodded, "It's settled then." Before he could go further, a well-dressed black man appeared. His speech was that of a well-educated individual, "Jonah, Moses."

The two men beamed. "Otis! How are you doing?" Hands were shaken and backs slapped good-naturedly.

Otis had been a slave and servant of the Governor of Antigua's family. He was on the ship that was taken by pirates, along with Cooper Cain and David MacArthur. Like Cain and MacArthur, Otis had gone aboard the pirate ship as a volunteer. It had soon become obvious that Otis didn't fit in with the pirates, due to his manners and education. The captain, Eli Taylor, was quick to recognize Otis's talents. Therefore, in a city where there were many businesses owned and operated by free men of color, Otis was made general manager of Hotel Provincial. He had made the overland trip from Savannah to New Orleans with Jonah and Moses when they'd escorted the Taylors and Cooper Cain back to the city.

When he got through shaking hands with his friends, Otis looked at Moses. "I know you are here with Jackson, so your free time will be limited. I'd consider it an honor though, Moses, if you would be my guest in my home. You will have your own room and the comfort of coming and going as you please. I have two housekeepers that will take care of your needs." This was said with a wink that Jonah didn't miss. "Also, when the two of you have time, I'd like to introduce you to our battalion of free men of color."

"That'd be great, Otis," both men replied.

"I'll take you up on your offer of hospitality," Moses added.

"My, where are my manners. You have to be Anastasia. May I welcome you, not only to the Hotel Provincial, but to the Crescent City, as well?"

Everyone had just gotten moved in and Jonah was thinking of a nap when there was a knock at his door. "Damnation," Jonah hissed. The hotel bellboy must have heard Jonah's outburst, as he seemed very cowed when the door was opened.

"I was told to await your response, suh."

Jonah tore open the envelope and after reading the letter, he handed it to Ana. They were invited to a reception to honor General Jackson and a select few of his staff, to be given at the home of Mr. and Mrs. Edward Livingston.

"Of course, we will attend," Ana replied and hunting for a writing quill and ink, she answered the invitation stating they would attend. "I wonder how they knew where to locate us," Ana thought aloud. She then looked at Jonah as if to say, 'well!'

"I told the general's aide, Captain Reid, where I intended to bivouac."

"Humph...bivouac. You call this bivouac?" Ana inquired.

Smiling, Jonah pulled her close. "Do you like it, Mademoiselle Greenville?"

For an answer, Ana looked into Jonah's eyes, "You truly love me, don't you, Jonah? Even after all that's happened to me, you love me... knowing that..."

Now it was Jonah who cutoff her words as he kissed her. "Do you really want to take a nap, Jonah?"

"Not if you have something better in mind," he said slyly. Saying that, he kissed her on the neck.

"I do," Ana replied.

"You do?"

"Yes... I need a dress for the reception."

Jonah's reaction made Ana laugh. He flopped back and sat on the edge of the bed. She pushed him back as she passionately kissed him. "But that can wait until after..."

CHAPTER TEN

THE NEXT WEEK WAS a blur. Ignoring an attack of dysentery, Jackson drove himself and those under his command. All week Jackson, along with Jonah in tow, toured the city's defenses. Fifty miles below the city was Fort Saint Phillip.

Jackson commented, "This is the key to preventing Admiral Cochrane and his navy from sailing right up to the city." He called to Major Butler, "We need to reinforce the fort. Make it so that it will be too costly to pass. We need additional batteries around the bend at…"

"English Turn," Captain Reid filled in.

The day after touring Fort Saint Phillip, Jackson sent Richard Smith to find the expected volunteers and to hurry them along. Edward Livingston and Jackson had both served in Congress together. As old friends, Jackson tended to listen to Livingston's counsel more than most of the other leaders in the city.

"Andy, you do not know how bad the friction is between the Creoles in the city and Claiborne's cronies. It's important you meet with them if you aim to get the support you need."

Looking at Jonah, Jackson asked, "Do you get the same feeling as Edward?"

"Yes, sir. There is a feeling, an insult, if you will, that the Creoles have been discounted," Jonah replied.

"Alright, set it up," Jackson said.

A reception at Place d'Armes was scheduled. If anyone could conciliate the Creoles, Jackson could. Bringing Ana to the reception proved to be fortuitous. The speech that Jackson gave had the hoped for results. Many of the leaders in the Creole community rushed forward. Ana was quick to translate the leaders' remarks for Jackson, since he was unable to speak the language.

Afterwards, Jackson thanked Ana and jokingly addressed his aides. "Gentlemen, meet the newest and most important member of my staff." This brought about the smiles Jackson knew it would do, following his remark. The general's remark made Ana beam. Jonah felt like Ana's ordeal was finally being pushed back into the recesses of her thoughts.

COMMODORE PATTERSON WAS IN agreement with Jackson that there was a huge potential for the British Navy to use Lake Borgne and its connecting waterways, Bayou Catalan or De Pecheurs at the head of the lake as a means to attack the city. Therefore, six gunboats under the command of Lieutenant Thomas Jones were sent to watch for the expected British forces. Jackson did not expect Jones to defeat the British Navy. But if he could just delay them and buy Jackson some time to set up the city's defenses, then the sacrifice of the boats would have been worth it.

"I understand that you were with Commodore Perry at Lake Erie," Patterson quizzed Jonah.

"Yes, sir. I was," Jonah replied.

"Would you like to put in a little sea time with Lieutenant Jones?" Patterson asked.

Before Jonah could reply, Jackson interrupted, "Jonah, no doubt, would take you up on your offer, Commodore, but unfortunately, I have a more urgent need for Jonah." Patterson nodded and dropped the subject.

Back at his headquarters on Royal Street, Jackson and several of the city's leaders went over a map of the land and waterways surrounding the city.

"It would seem that we have done all that we can," one of Jackson's aides commented.

"No, we haven't." This came from one of the Creoles with better English than most. "We have many bayous feeding off the rivers and lakes that lead right into the city. We need to render them impassable as much as we can." Jackson nodded, agreeing with the man's advice.

Ax men were then sent to fell trees and block the bayous so that an amphibious assault using the waterways could be prevented.

"We are running out of men," an exhausted Jackson admitted. He had worked with abandon to set up their defenses on a city that was virtually wide open.

"You still have men at your disposal, Andy."

Jackson looked at the speaker, Edward Livingston, and then at Jonah, who added, "He's right, General."

"You are referring to those pirates, I suppose," Jackson said. The general leaned back in his chair. "I made my statements based on Claiborne's words that I'd never accept the pirate. How can I go back on my word?"

Livingston cleared his throat, "What if he was no longer considered a pirate, General?"

"How can that be?" Jackson asked.

"Amnesty," Livingston threw out. "I believe that I have the votes needed to get it through the state legislature."

Jackson nodded his head. "That would work."

"We have the reception at your house tomorrow, Edward," Jackson continued. "After that, we can meet in secret with LaFitte. Jonah, you will be my aide. I don't want this to go any further. Set up the meeting, Edward, but the rascal is to come alone," Jackson said.

"Yes sir, I will see to it," Edward replied.

A reception had been planned for Jackson at the home of Edward Livingston; the night after Jackson agreed to meet LaFitte. Jonah and

Ana arrived in the hotel's barouche. As the carriage pulled up, a lone rider on a magnificent white horse rode up.

Recognizing Jackson, Jonah whispered to Ana, "Wonder where he got that mount?"

"Isn't he dressed so splendid?" Ana responded. Whereas Jonah was looking at the horse, Ana was looking at the man.

Jackson had discarded his worn and washed out uniform and in its place was the full dress uniform of a major general. The uniform was a blue frock coat with buff facings and gold lace, a white waistcoat, white tight-fitting breeches, and boots that reached above the knees. He was a most impressing figure. He'd cut a fine swath with the ladies in that get up. Jonah had never seen Jackson dressed in such an imposing manner. Undoubtedly, some tailor and his minions had been working hard to turn out such splendid attire. *Wonder who he wants to impress*, Jonah suddenly thought, the ladies or a pirate. It dawned on Jonah that his invitation, along with Jackson's arrival alone must mean the meeting had been set and was tonight.

"Ana!"

"Yes, dear."

"I believe you may have to return to the hotel alone after the reception. But don't worry; I will follow as soon as I can."

A fear went through Ana, and she grasped Jonah's hands so tightly that he could feel her nails.

Jonah continued, "It's nothing dangerous, my love. Seeing the general alone makes me think there will be a meeting tonight that's not for public knowledge. You wait up for me if you want to." Being coy then, he let his hand slide across her breast and he helped her down the steps that the driver had set out. Without speaking, Ana gave him a knowing look.

Livingston's doorman ushered Jonah and Ana in. He quickly returned to the door to escort Jackson in. The general had paused to speak with the groomsman, who took the reins on his horse. Livingston rushed to greet Jackson and presented him to Madam Livingston.

Mrs. Livingston, a Creole, suddenly turned pale and began fanning herself; she was so taken by Jackson. The room was full of young belles and they were all in awe at the tall, slender man.

Livingston then turned to the ladies, "Mademoiselles, I have the honor to present Major General Andrew Jackson of the United States Army."

The general bowed and Mrs. Livingston took Jackson's hand and introduced him to each of the young ladies. Jonah leaned over and whispered to Ana, "Jackson is smiling because he hasn't a clue as to what's being said, since it's all in French."

As the evening wore on, Jackson made small talk with the ladies. Sometimes, Eliza Choturd translated, and on a few occasions Ana served as translator. Soon dinner was served. Over the meal, the conversation drifted to a new painting of Mrs. Livingston's by artist Michael Benton.

"He is the talk of all the young ladies. You must stand in line to be painted by this talented wonder. Have you met him yet, dear?" Mrs. Livingston asked Ana.

"No, I've not had the pleasure," Ana replied.

"Well, you simply must. Did Edward not say you were staying at Hotel Provincial?"

"Yes, Captain Taylor and his wife were gracious enough to allow us to stay in their residence until New Orleans is secured."

Leaning over and darting her eyes left and then right, and assuring herself that no one was listening, Mrs. Livingston whispered, "I've been told that's where LaFitte stays when he's in town. Hmm...what a man, my dear, any number of the town's more established ladies would kick their fat arsed husbands out of their lives for just a night alone with M'sieur LaFitte."

Smiling, Ana asked, "Madam included?"

Smiling back at Ana, Ms. Livingston winked and replied, "I'll never tell."

They were talking about her painting by M'sieur Benton, when Jonah walked up. "It's time for me to go, Ana. Mr. Livingston has provided an extra escort to see you home." Ana only nodded her head.

Mrs. Livingston shook her head, "Our men playing soldiers. I will go with you to your home." Smiling again, she whispered, "I want to know if this man of yours is really the president's man."

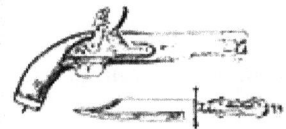

CHAPTER ELEVEN

A MISTY FOG LAY LOW over the muddy streets of New Orleans. Ana and Mrs. Livingston sat in the cab of the barouche with a blanket over them to keep out the chill. Louis, the driver, had a cloak over him as he sat in the driver's seat. He expertly handled the carriage and horse through the narrow Crescent City streets.

One hundred identical blocks made up the city. Most of the houses on each side of the street were two-story and similar in construction. Although, they were very plain on the outside, a number of them were plush and richly furnished on the inside. Most of the houses had wrought iron rails around the second floor balconies. The driver, Louis', eyes were on a semi nude woman being undressed by her husband or lover with little concern of who may be observing their tryst.

When the horse stopped suddenly and reared up, Louis was almost thrown from the driver's box. The ladies were hurled forward, bouncing against the carriage walls. Standing in the intersection was a group of six men. The dim coach lantern was enough for Louis to make out the evil looking lot. Each man wore a bandana to cover his face but their greasy hair and dirty beards were plainly visible. All of them were heavily armed with sabers and pistols. Louis reached for the coach gun but a shot rang out and the ball tore into his shoulder, burning the flesh like a red-hot poker.

"Careful, nigger, or the next will be through your gut," a red-headed thief called out. "Who's inside the carriage?" the red-head asked, obviously the leader of the bunch.

"Just my mistress and a friend," Louis replied, his hand now bloody from holding his shoulder wound.

Red-head motioned to a man, who snatched the carriage door open. "Out," he snapped.

The women stepped out as ordered. Although the women were dressed in formal gowns that almost reached their ankles, they were low cut, off-the-shoulder affairs with deep cut clefts that showed high, proud breasts. The sight caused the rogue to be aroused instantly. These were not the usual tavern wenches he was used to associating with. The diamond necklace and rings did nothing to distract his sudden lust.

"Would you look at these wenches?" he called out. "You can have the jewels; I'm for a bit of quim."

Mistaking them for some of Jean LaFitte's smugglers, Mrs. Livingston spoke out, "I must warn you, my husband and Jean LaFitte are good friends."

"Sod LaFitte," the red-headed man hissed. "We go our own way." Stepping to the coach door, he looked at the women. "I believe you're right, Lester, these are two handsome wenches." Saying this, he reached up and roughly tore the lace that covered Ana's cleavage away. "We will pleasure ourselves with these two until we tire of them and then we'll dump them in the bayou."

"I wouldn't," a voice rang out, along with the metallic click of hammers being cocked on pistols. Richard Smith was returning from an errand for Jackson when he'd heard the shot that wounded Louis. He carried two double-barrel saddle pistols. Very quietly he had approached the intersection. If the men had taken the jewels, he would have let them ride off rather than risk either of the two women getting hurt. But that was all changed now. "Move along and we'll forget this happened," Smith said in a strong, no nonsense voice.

"Like hell," Red-head yelled and reached for his pistol.

Smartly, Ana grabbed Mrs. Livingston and jerked her to the ground as the sound of gunfire broke the silent night. Red-head's shot plucked Smith's cloak while Smith's ball went true. The rogue's shirt turned crimson where Smith's ball struck him square in the chest. Falling, he hit Lester, whose aim was thrown off, but a snap shot from Smith entered his throat…two men down.

Sensing the opportunity, Louis grabbed the coach gun and shot another thief in the back. Three down. Two of the remaining rogues charged Smith, making his horse jump. It saved one man's life, but as he was being pulled from his horse, Smith jammed his pistol into a man and pulled the trigger. The ball went into the fleshy part between the collarbones and traveled to the lungs. Blood filled the man's mouth as he choked on his own blood.

As Smith fell from his horse, he managed to pull his hunting knife out. As he rolled in the muddy street with his attacker, he felt a searing sensation as the man's saber sliced into the muscle in his upper arm. Knowing if the man broke free, he'd have the advantage with the longer blade; Smith gripped the man with all his strength. The man struggled to get loose but Smith's knife rose and fell, once, twice, and a third time. Each time the knife plunged into the thief, his struggle became less until the man became limp.

The last man had attacked Louis, who used the carriage whip, lashing out, and striking his foe in the face. When the man's hands went to his eyes, Louis quickly pulled the blade from his sword cane and lunged downward, driving the blade between the ribs and deep into his chest. The thief fell backwards, causing a sucking sound as the blade was pulled free.

Smith rose as Louis climbed down from the driver's box…bloody but victorious. Six dead men lay in the street. The women were getting up off the ground as a crowd gathered around.

"Send for a doctor," Ana shouted.

"And the law," Mrs. Livingston added.

Ana was relieved; she had decided she'd kill herself rather than be abused as she had in the past. *Damn Jonah*, she thought, but then quickly changed her mind. He would have fought and likely could be lying on the ground with the thieves. She was glad that he hadn't been there. By the time the doctor got there, Louis was in a bad way. Loss of blood and pain had made him faint.

"Him first," Smith ordered the doctor.

The doctor had never treated a black man before but something in the tall man's voice let him know there'd be no argument. Once the doctor had done all he could do on the street, another of the Livingston's servants arrived with a wagon as he had received word to do. A mattress and blankets were in the back. Louis was lifted and put on the mattress. Grimacing in pain, he did not cry out. Mrs. Livingston rode on the wagon seat and Smith drove the barouche on to the Hotel Provincial.

There, a second doctor, who'd been summoned, removed the temporary dressings, cleaned and sewed up the saber cut. "It was not too deep," he said, "so you should recover soon. Just keep the wound clean so that ill humors, which are so prevalent in the city, do not take hold."

By the time the doctor left, Moses and Otis had arrived, having been notified by one of the hotel staff. "You will probably be safe here tonight," Otis said, "but you never know when some of the gang's kin or friends might be out for revenge. We'll set a guard. You can sleep on a bed in my office, if you like."

By this time, Tim and Donnie were out. "Boring as it's been lately, I wouldn't mind shooting some villain," Donnie snorted.

Otis got a glass of brandy for Smith. "To help you sleep," he said, as he passed the glass to him.

Thankful, Smith gulped the fiery liquid down. As Moses helped with his boots, Smith laid gently back on the cot and was quickly asleep.

Moses then walked with Ana to her suite. "I will be by the doors, Ana. You rest. The only man that will pass through them tonight will be Jonah."

Placing her arm on the big man's shoulder, she smiled, "I shall rest knowing that I will be safe."

As she walked off, Moses could only guess at the terror that she'd experienced. *Damn Jonah*, he thought. *He should have made sure I was there to protect his woman.* Though she hadn't mentioned it, Moses knew Ana would never allow herself to be taken again…not alive. *Had it not been for Smith*…Moses shuddered when he thought of it. *Well, Jonah is going to get a piece of my mind. That is a fact.* He pulled up a chair and a footstool and sat next to the French doors leading to the patio. He was there when Jonah came in and found a pistol shoved into his gut. A cold voice hissed, "If you ain't Jonah, you are a dead man."

"It's me, Moses," Jonah cried out.

"I know. I just wanted to scare you…put the fear of God into you. Now, have a seat and let's talk."

Jonah swallowed hard, "Is Ana safe?"

"She is now, brother. I'll light a candle while you pour us a drink."

Standing outside, Donnie watched. He'd recognized Jonah when he was dropped off. *Might should have told him to speak out*, he thought. *Oh well! He didn't get kilt.*

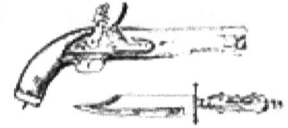

CHAPTER TWELVE

THE OLD ABSINTHE HOUSE sat on the corner of Bourbon Street and Bienville Street. On the corner of Charles Street and Chartres Street, not too far away, a man ran up to a building that had a sign proclaiming it to be Maspero's Coffee House.

"They are there, boss," the man said, speaking to Jean LaFitte.

"Just the two of them?" LaFitte asked.

"Three, if you count Mr. Livingston," the runner replied.

LaFitte turned to his brother, Pierre. "Stay back and out of sight. If this turns out to be a trap, you know what to do." Pierre merely nodded.

LaFitte rode to the meeting place in a carriage. As the driver pulled up in front of the Old Absinthe House, Lafitte got out. Upon entering the door, he was met by Livingston, and the two walked up the stairs. When LaFitte walked into the upstairs room, he was introduced to Jackson. He had previously met Jonah Lee, and knew that Jonah was President Madison's special agent.

Jonah spoke as he shook LaFitte's hand, "It's good to see you again, sir."

Smiling, LaFitte said, "Yes, I remember you. We were introduced by Captain Taylor and his young friend, Cooper Cain."

"Yes sir. It's good of you to remember."

"I understand from Mr. Livingston that you are the president's man."

"Just an observer," Jonah responded. Thankfully, LaFitte let it drop.

Jackson, not sure what he was expecting LaFitte to be like, soon found himself impressed. Instead of the rough pirate the governor had painted a picture of, Jackson found LaFitte to be well-mannered, well-dressed, and of impeccable behavior. Quickly, his guard was down and he found himself liking the man. Over the next hour, LaFitte outlined the communication between himself and the British Navy. How he'd reached out to the governor, only to have it thrown back in his face. To make matters worse, the damnable fool of a governor had added insult to injury by allowing Commodore Patterson to raid Barataria and steal a great amount of LaFitte's property.

Hearing this, Livingston added, "General, M'sieur LaFitte had at his disposal enough ships and men to destroy Patterson, but rather than fire on a United States ship, he and his men fled. Had he chose to ally himself with the British general, New Orleans would now be under their control."

Jackson took all this information in. Clearing his throat, Jackson spoke, "It appears that I was a bit hasty in my previous remarks."

LaFitte waved it away. "They were made believing our esteemed governor, sir." The sarcasm was not lost on Jackson.

"Yes, but once spoken, they are hard to undo," Jackson replied. "Mr. Livingston, however, has assured me that this week a recommendation for amnesty will be brought forward."

Nodding, Livingston said, "I'm assured that the President of the Senate, Fulwar Skipwith, and Speaker of the House, Magloire Guichard, have the votes to pass the amnesty."

"When this happens," Jackson said, "I will be free to change my mind and publicly shake your hand in friendship and accept your help for our glorious cause." As an afterthought, he then added, "By the way, Mr. LaFitte, young Jonah told me in no uncertain terms several weeks ago that I was a jackass for not accepting your offer."

Jonah flushed, "I don't think that I said that, General."

"Close enough. It's what you meant," Jackson replied.

Suddenly, both LaFitte and Livingston realized there was far more to Jonah Lee than met the casual observer's eye.

Turning to Livingston, Jackson said, "Unless there's anything else, gentlemen, we should call this meeting to an end. I expect to see you both as quickly as the amnesty is passed. I have dire need of your advice and resources, Mr. LaFitte."

"I will not let you down, General."

"I never thought that you would, sir."

BREAKFAST THE NEXT MORNING consisted of fried or scrambled cheese eggs, buttered grits or fried potatoes, bacon or sugar cured ham, hot buttered biscuits, chicory coffee, hot chocolate or milk. If you were still hungry after that, local honey or fig preserves could grace your biscuit. Beignets were also available.

Richard Smith was helped to the breakfast table by Donnie and Tim. Jonah and Ana, followed by Moses, had just made their way to the kitchen table when they heard a horse draw up beyond the open kitchen door. A rider in uniform entered the kitchen through the open door. The feast laid out on the table made the rider touch his stomach as he let out an involuntary groan, "Mmm."

Jonah, rose up smiling, "Morning, Lieutenant. Would you care to join us?"

"I wouldn't want to put you out of the way, sir."

"Nonsense, you can see there's plenty."

"Thank you, sir," the young lieutenant said, hanging his hat on the back of a chair as he sat down.

Seeing the exchange, Otis, who'd been standing at the door watching the other guests in the dining room, quickly ordered a setting for the lieutenant. He then resumed his observation of the hotel's guests as several of the tables were full.

Coming down the stairs, into the dining room, was the artist, Mike Benton. He was a tall man with thick black hair and a gray beard. Before he could be seated, Otis stepped into the dining room and called to him, "Good morning, sir." Benton nodded his head in acknowledgement.

"I wonder if I might have a moment, sir." Again Benton nodded and Otis continued, "This way, please."

Leading Benton into the kitchen, Otis cleared his throat, getting everyone's attention. "It is my pleasure to introduce, Mr. Michael Benton, an artist of no small talent."

Ana rose up quickly. "I have seen a sample of your work at Mr. Livingston's home. You are, as our host says, a man of considerable talent."

Otis introduced Ana. "Miss Anastasia Greenville, Mr. Benton."

"My pleasure, Miss Greenville, you are a rare beauty."

Jonah spoke up, "One that I'd like for you to capture on canvas, sir."

"It would be a pleasure, sir, if we can agree on a suitable time. I have several commissions already in the making. I only have scheduled sittings at night. I had hoped to capture some sketches of a battle taking place," Benton said.

Before Benton could speak any further, the lieutenant paused between bites, "That might be sooner than you think. We've just gotten word that the British have destroyed our gunboats on Lake Borgne. The general sent me to fetch you to headquarters as soon as it is convenient for you, Mr. Lee," the lieutenant added. It appeared the lieutenant had felt that 'as soon as it is convenient' meant after breakfast.

"Thank you, Lieutenant," Jonah replied.

Gulping down his last swallow of coffee, Moses volunteered, "Are you coming, Mr. Smith?"

"Yes, but I'll be a few minutes."

As Moses nodded his understanding, Benton asked, "May I be allowed to join you, gentlemen?"

"Why not," Jonah answered. Old Hickory might like the idea of being painted during a battle.

Jackson's headquarters was in a buzz. By the time, Jonah was shown into the general's meeting; Lieutenant Jones was finishing his report. "Admiral Cochrane lowered forty-five attack barges, each armed with cannon. The sides were planked up so that the crews would have some protection from our muskets. The same officer that had talked to Mr. LaFitte, a Captain Lockyer, appeared to be in command. It was the morning of December 14th that they attacked. The wind was against the British. Right off, the flagship and one of their gunboats was grounded. Thinking that I might inflict some punishment on the British, I decided to fight it out. I was hoping it might make it difficult for them to land their troops if I could destroy some of the barges, and buy you some time, General." Jones paused a moment, and then continued his narrative, "These barges were not your usual barge, General. One of my men counted eighty men climbing off the flagship down into the barge. We gave them our all, General. We lost about a third of our men, six were killed and about thirty-five were wounded. We sank several of the barges, and killed near a hundred men. There were several officers among the dead. I know Captain Lockyer was severely wounded when his barge tried to board one of our gunboats. As soon as it was obvious that we'd done all we could do, sir, I discontinued the action and hightailed it back here to report. It is my sad duty to report, sir; the British now control the waterways."

Jackson went over to a map hanging on a wall. Voices were heard greeting a new arrival. Turning to see who had entered, Jackson spoke to Mr. Smith, "I see you are up and about. I hope your wound was not serious." *Damn, is there anything the general doesn't know about*, thought Jonah.

"I'm well enough for duty," Smith replied.

"Good," Jackson responded, as he turned back to the map. "I want you to ride to the Port of Petites Cosquilles." Jackson said this thumbing a place on the map. "Tell Captain Newman he's in charge of our artillery there and he is ordered to defend his post to the last extremity."

The room grew very quiet and still, after hearing Jackson's order. It was, in fact, very likely death warrant.

"In case he is unable to hold on," Jackson said in a firm voice, "he is to spike the guns and blow up the fort."

"Yes, sir."

"You will then take letters to General Coffee, General Carroll, and General Thomas informing them of the loss of our gunboats. Let them know that I'm in dire need of their troops. They are strongly urged to use all possible speed in marching their troops to New Orleans."

"Yes, General," was all Smith said.

"Good man," Jackson said. "See my secretary for the letters and then be off...and Richard."

"Yes sir."

"We all appreciate your efforts in doing away with the rogues that attacked our dear lady friends. Had you not dispatched them so effectively last night, I would have had them shot this morning."

"Thank you, sir."

"No. We thank you, Richard."

-

That afternoon, Jackson was informed that the LaFittes had been granted amnesty. He met with Jean LaFitte, for the first time, that evening where he publicly shook hands with him and welcomed the smuggler into his fold. Pierre became part of the general's staff, and Dominique Youx was given command of a battery of cannons. *He should*, Jonah thought. The cannons, and the men, belong to the LaFittes. Jonah's thought continued, *I wonder if the meeting held last night will ever become known about. 'No matter,'* he said to himself. *Thanks to Mr. Livingston, it has all worked out.* As men were sent out on errands, Jackson's office became less crowded.

Taking advantage of the lull, Jonah took Benton in tow and walked up to Jackson. "General, I'd like for you to meet Mr. Michael Benton. He is interested in capturing battle scenes on canvas, for history's sake, so that generations to come will be able to see what you've done for our glorious cause."

Jackson shook Benton's hand. "So you desire to preserve our cause by painting battle scenes, do you?"

"Yes sir, so that our children and their children will be able to see what we've done to keep our nation sovereign."

"Well good, sir. I welcome you to the fold," Jackson replied. He thought, *it can't hurt to have our victories put on canvas*. It also wouldn't hurt to use them as a political ploy if he decided to run for office. If they were victorious…if not…Jackson didn't want to think about that possibility.

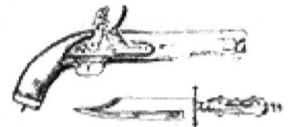

CHAPTER THIRTEEN

THE BRITISH BARGES RETURNED to Admiral Cochrane's flagship, *Tennant*. They had succeeded in their mission but at a heavy loss. Lake Borgne belonged to the British and they now had smaller vessels to land their army. Heavy rains greeted the British as they attempted to deploy the army. Many of the British ships found themselves grounded in the shallows of the lake. Due to this, the army landed on the swampy Pine Island without the benefit of tents or any means of shelter.

In addition to the misery created by the weather, Pine Island abounded in snakes and alligators, not to mention the horde of biting insects. As the sun sank, the temperature fell with it, and a severe frost set in. By morning, a large number of the Negro volunteers from the West Indies, who'd never experienced such conditions, were now dead. Realizing the blunder, the British pushed on. It was now or never. They had to engage Jackson's army, which was rumored to be twenty thousand men.

So it was that one bayou, Bayou Bienvenue, which had been overlooked by Jackson's men, became a route for the British forces to march to dry land just below the city without being detected.

SHORTLY AFTER LAFITTE WAS pardoned with Livingston's encouragement, Jackson accepted the offer of Barataria's privateers' services. A large corps under the command of Captains Dominique Youx and Renato Beluche were employed. The new volunteers brought with them powder, shot, cannons, and small arms, war supplies that

Jackson had been critically short of. A letter went out to free men of color to volunteer. Now, all classes of society were volunteering their service.

In a moment alone with Ana, Jonah admitted that he'd never seen anyone equal Jackson's ability to unify people to stand and fight. No matter what color, age, or sex, the population of New Orleans now stood together defiant of the British for invading their shores. The ranks swelled with volunteers. Jackson, in addition to his one thousand regulars, also had four or five thousand militia. Hopefully, more would arrive soon.

THE FOLLOWING MORNING, JONAH and Moses, as guests of Otis, went out to review the two battalions of free men of color. Otis, with little fighting experience except for his short foray as a pirate with Jonah's friend, Cooper Cain, was nonetheless commissioned as a major. Jonah was sure it had more to do with Otis's education and ability to organize than anything else. However, Jonah had no doubt Otis would fight.

As they rode up to the bivouac, they were greeted by a young black boy carrying a drum, "Morning, Majah."

"Jordan," Otis responded with a nod. "Gentlemen, this is Jordan Noble. He swears his drums will beat the roll for the entire time that we fight the Redcoats."

Jonah and Moses followed Otis's example and swung down from their mounts. The grinning youth stepped forward with an outstretched hand, "Proud to meet'cha," he said. After shaking Jonah and Moses' hands, he led the group off with a drum roll.

Moses leaned over and whispered to Jonah, "He's letting the troops know an officer is here so that they can tidy up any soldier shenanigans. He ain't got me fooled. He was sent here to watch."

Smiling at Moses' words, Jonah could not disagree. However, he couldn't help but think of the boy's words, 'I'll beat the roll till those Redcoats are kicked back to the sea.' For some reason, he had a thought he couldn't explain, but he believed the boy. He believed that when the battle started, little Jordan Noble would be there with his drum. The boy would also be there when the final shot was fired as well. An omen...who knew, but Jonah decided that he'd put his money on the boy. It came to him then that the boy had the same determined attitude as Andy 'by God' Jackson. From the top man to the least little drummer boy, they lived the spirit of 'we shall be victorious.'

The review was much like any other military review. The battalion was made up of about three hundred fifty men. The senior sergeants were men who'd fought in the Revolutionary War and the Indian War. They were no nonsense veterans. Only a few of the officers had a uniform of sorts. Otis, being one of a few, was dressed out with a patch on his shoulder proclaiming him to be in the Second Battalion of the Free Men of Color Militia. The senior enlisted men wore a sash of green around the waist identifying them as sergeants. While the review was impressive, it was quickly apparent that these men, who were ready to fight and die, lacked the most important...the most necessary component of all for being a soldier...weapons. Fewer than half of the men of the two battalions had a firearm of any type.

When asked about the lack of firearms, Otis just shrugged. "We are doing the best that we can. We have set it up so that our best shots will do the firing and have two, maybe three, rifles while behind him others will load for him. If it gets to hand-to-hand, they all have knives and field machetes."

The ride back to the city gave Jonah time to think. Brave men were willing to fight and die to protect their city. There was no other place in America quite like New Orleans. The city was beautiful, but was it all a mask? The city was below sea level. Beautiful moss filled majestic oak trees that lined the entrances to huge, columned plantation homes. The pastures were filled with thoroughbred horses. There were also the wonderful hotels and restaurants, even the bawdy houses and gambling dens. They all lived in danger. If the dikes broke, the city would be lost. The river and the sea would flood the land. Did the British realize just how precarious the situation was? They could destroy the city much easier than by taking it, Jonah realized. But what was their motive in plundering the city or taking it as a foothold to their southern campaign? Were he the British commander, Jonah knew what he'd do. Destroy the dikes and all opposition would be gone. He'd then use his forces to overwhelm and take either Pensacola or Mobile. A shiver went over Jonah. *You're a ruthless sod*, he thought to himself. *Hopefully, the British commander doesn't think along the same lines I do. If so, all will be lost.*

Dinner that evening was at the attorney Meeks' home. Ana and Meeks' wife, Carolyn, had hit it off pretty well. They seemed to enjoy each other's company. Several of the town's upper society was there also, including Cindy Veigh, Major Gabriel Villeres, Commodore Patterson, and Edward Livingston, the man, who had set up the secret meeting between Jackson and the pirate, Jean LaFitte. Jackson was also there in a dress uniform that hung loosely on his tall frame. He looked pale and hollow-eyed, but his voice still carried the fire of command.

Later that evening, Ana asked, "Have you noticed the absence of Governor Claiborne at most of the events and dinners that we've attended?"

"Aye," Jonah replied, using his friend, Cooper Cain's, nautical response. He then added, "Commodore Patterson was much too verbal about smashing LaFitte's stronghold at Grand Terre tonight. LaFitte's men did not fire a shot in return. Had LaFitte ordered it, I'm sure. Patterson would have been defeated soundly. Did you hear Jackson comment about the attack?" Jonah asked Ana.

When she shook her head no, Jonah suddenly lost his train of thought as he watched her unbutton the top of her dress, allowing her ample bosom to come into view. When Jonah didn't continue, Ana looked up at him. Seeing where his attention was centered, Ana pulled her top back together. "Go on, you lecherous devil."

Jonah smiled, bent forward and kissed Ana on the forehead. After kissing Ana, Jonah continued his story, "Jackson told Patterson it sounded like a hollow victory when the man they needed to help defend the city never put up any defense. Jackson asked him, 'What about the spoils? Have they been returned to the rightful owners? They have been given amnesty, after all.' 'The amnesty didn't occur until after the attack,' Patterson responded, trying to defend his actions. 'Who did the "spoils" go to then?' Jackson inquired, knowing full well Patterson and his men kept everything that was worth taking. 'Was the bounty turned over to the governor, the city, or state?' Jackson pressed him. Patterson mumbled, not yet. 'And not likely to be,' one of the wives said. The commodore soon made his departure, citing early morning duty."

"Probably going to hide his ill gotten gains," Ana said, as she returned to undressing herself.

Hmm, maybe tonight would be a night for me to enjoy my gains, Jonah thought. Watching his woman undress in the low candlelight, with her silhouette against the far wall enhancing his mood, Jonah realized just how much this woman moved him. He was suddenly impatient, and ready for the battle, the war, to be over so that he could go home... go back to Georgia and get married. He wanted to get married, have children, get fat, and grow old sitting on the porch of their home.

Ana blew out the candle, breaking his reverie. "You coming to bed?" she asked.

Using Cain's term again, he replied, "Aye, a whole battalion of Redcoats couldn't keep me from what promise awaits me between your sheets, Madam."

Smiling, Ana said, "Talk. I don't want to hear you talk. I want to see you in action."

"You'll not have but a moment to wait, my lady. Not more than a moment."

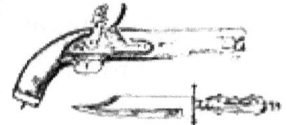

CHAPTER FOURTEEN

THE BRITISH COMMANDER, VICE Admiral Cochrane, walked the quarterdeck of his flagship. It was a cloudless day and a bright sun was shining down. A man stood in the chains taking steady soundings. The soundings being called out by the leadsman indicated the depth of the water was shoaling fast.

Another cast of the lead line had the ship's captain growing nervous. "I'm afraid we must anchor, My Lord, or surely we will run aground."

"Very well," Lord Cochrane agreed. It was not the thing he wanted to do, but fate didn't always smile upon the Royal Navy. "Make the signal," Cochrane ordered.

The captain acknowledged his admiral and passed the word to the first lieutenant, who passed it to the signals midshipman. 'Ships to anchor, all captains repair on board the flagship.'

In regular order, the fleet captains brought their ships up into the wind and dropped anchor. The lakes had been cleared of the American gunboats. Now all the launches, barges, and pinnaces of the fleet were ordered to be gathered together. The barges had been made specifically for the assault on the American gunboats and then as a means to land troops for the assault on New Orleans. Including the gigs from *HMS Tennant* and *Seahorse*, the British had put together forty craft. Each of the craft mounted forward guns. When all the craft shoved off they carried over a thousand men. Men who were ready to attack the city of New Orleans.

IN THE CITY OF New Orleans, Jackson, tired and worn down, watched his number of men to defend the city grow. Captain Pierre Jugeant, a half-breed Choctaw Indian, was authorized to levy and form companies of all the Choctaw Indians he could collect. As per the secret meeting with LaFitte, the privateers had all been released from jail and joined General Jackson's forces. Knowing the assistance of these men…men, who had actually tasted the din of battles, would be most beneficial, Jackson welcomed them into the fold. A corps was formed under the command of Dominique Youx and Renato Beluche. They would be employed along the lines where their experience and skills were needed the most. They'd be in command of the twenty-four pound cannons of Batteries Number Three and Four. The rest of the privateers would be put in one of three other companies of marines.

Word was sent to General Winchester in Mobile informing him of the loss of the American gunboats and an attack by the British was to be expected at any time. Jackson recommended to Winchester to use the greatest vigilance in case the British attacked the town and come overland to New Orleans.

Jackson then penned letters to the Secretary of War. He informed the secretary that none of the promised troops from Tennessee or Kentucky had arrived yet. He also told him that he would establish martial law. The city shall be defended, Jackson stated. There was no need to add the statement, since the secretary knew that Jackson would give his all.

The people of New Orleans were informed by Jackson's scouts that the enemy was now within striking distance and that an attack could come at any minute. Yet the city's occupants remained calm. They pursued their usual occupations and continued to enjoy their nightlife activities, except for when they were interrupted to perform some military related duty.

It seemed that it was now common knowledge that Jonah was the 'president's man.' He was on every invitation list that was sent out, frequently along with General Jackson. As they could not attend all of the social events that they were invited to, Jonah left the response to the events they'd attend or sadly have to decline, up to Ana. She seemed to be a stalwart at such doings so much so that Jackson had allowed her to attend to his event calendar on occasion. But how much longer would that continue? Jonah was truthful with his woman — the British were close and they could expect an attack at anytime. The question in the Jackson camp was only from what direction. Scouts were sent out daily. Every possible route was being watched, or so they believed. *Where are the reinforcements?* Jackson wondered. *Will I be eternally short of trained fighting men?*

AT THE HOTEL PROVINCIAL, the evening meal had been served. Most of the men moved off to play cards. Donnie, Tim, and Scrap were back together for a short time. Each had been deployed, scouting for approaches to the city that the enemy might use. Moses went off with Otis; Lucy and Fawn had taken to making themselves scarce after meeting up with some of LaFitte's men. No one seemed to mind. Captain Steve Lieupo and Richard Smith had dined frequently with Jonah and Ana. The talk was always pleasant and the impending British invasion was kept out of the conversation.

The hotel's chef had performed a minor miracle with tonight's meal. He had prepared a roast duck with caramelized onions, sweet potatoes with a buttery pecan topping, green beans, and a cup of peeled and sliced oranges. A fresh loaf of warm bread was devoured with a creamy butter. For dessert, the chef had prepared a bourbon chocolate pecan pie and, if the guests preferred, beignets were available. Each dessert was served with a cup of chicory coffee, black or with cream. With full stomachs, the men retired to the courtyard to fire up their cigars. Ana promised that she'd be there after she freshened up.

A waiter brought out a decanter of brandy. "We have a fine sherry if the lady would like an after dinner drink," the man offered. Jonah nodded that she would.

With Ana inside the hotel, the conversation quickly turned to the war. Richard Smith raised his glass in a toast, "You know how to fight a war, Jonah."

Smiling, Captain Lieupo said, "It has not always been like this."

"No, Steve, Horseshoe Bend was nothing like this, was it? It was cold, hard ground when it wasn't wet."

Nodding, Steve moved to avoid a flying bug. His limp was very visible. Seeing Smith notice the limp, Lieupo explained, "Red Stick arrow in my hip, played hell getting it out. I would not have made it if not for Jonah, Moses, and a scout named Henry Parrish." Smith didn't push the conversation when neither man offered more information.

"I do miss Henry," Jonah said. "Henry, Scrap, and the Halls, are all cut from the same cloth."

"Henry should be with General Coffee when he gets here," Lieupo replied.

"Which will hopefully be soon," Smith said. "The general, meaning Jackson, is fearful of an attack at any moment. He can't understand why they haven't been sighted yet."

At that moment, a streak of lightning flashed across the sky and thunder rolled. "We'd better be calling it an evening," Lieupo said, looking at the sky. Not a star could be seen.

Gulping down the last of his brandy, Smith agreed. "Tell Ana we had a pleasant evening."

Jonah watched as a livery boy brought his friends their horses. Another flash of lightning came. "You'd better hurry," he warned as Smith and Lieupo rode off.

Standing at the door, Ana called to the livery boy. "Lem, have you checked on Coco today?"

"Yes, Miz. Ana. That mule loves his apples and carrots. I think he needs a bit more exercise. He's getting fat."

"Do you want to ride him, Lem?"

"No, Madame. He ain't partial to me riding him."

"Me either," Jonah joined in. He knew Ana treated the beast like a hound dog.

THE RAIN BEGAN TO pour, not just a quick squall but a heavy downpour. Heavy rains such as the British soldiers getting out of the transport barges had never seen. The barges had run aground and troops that had been packed tightly into these vessels were tired and stiff. Now the rain, and to make it worse, their cloaks were drenched in minutes, offering no protection from the deluge. After ten hours in these boats, the British landed on a small spot of land called Pine Island, and not on Lake Borgne's banks. Pine Island was really more a spot of firm ground in the midst of a swamp. Other than a few stunted fir trees and scraggly shrubs, there were no trees.

As the army assembled, they could hear the grunts of alligators. Waterfowl took wing as the soldiers tramped up to the high ground, and cottonmouths slithered away as more and more men went up to firmer ground. They had no tents or huts for shelter. They also didn't have any dry wood for fires, and no warm clothing to protect them from the December frost that set in when the rain finally subsided. Not used to this cold, several of the negroes from the Caribbean Islands became exhausted and fell asleep, only to die before morning. It was a bad beginning. Demoralized by finding many of their friends had perished in their sleep, the fight was taken from many of the troops before the first shot was ever fired. Nevertheless, when the sun had risen and a sparse meal had been eaten, the British moved out. Marching through the swamp, the British made it within eight miles below the city of New Orleans before they were discovered.

JACKSON WAS IN GOOD spirits. It was like a Christmas gift had come early. Pierre LaFitte had just discovered five hundred muskets and seventy-five hundred badly needed flints.

"It's providence that you talked me into meeting with LaFitte," Jackson admitted to Jonah.

The LaFittes had come through on every promise, including providing cannons off-loaded from their ships. Jackson was so happy, he'd made the pirates part of his staff. A knock on the door caused both Jonah and the general to turn their attention toward the door. The door eased open and Jackson's aide, Captain Reid, poked his head in.

Jackson beckoned his aide in. "It must be good news, Jonah," he said. "Look how John is smiling."

"It is good news, sir. General Coffee has just been sighted."

"You're right, Captain. Come, my boy, let's put on a proper welcome." With that Jackson picked up his sword and hat. Not sure exactly who the 'my boy' was directed to, both Jonah and Captain Reid followed Jackson out the door.

It proved to be only the advance guard, but the rest would be there within a day, two at the most. "We came as soon as we could, General," Coffee said after dismounting his horse and saluting Jackson. After some pleasantries, Coffee said, "I see you still have Madison's spy in the midst." This was said with a smile.

"I see you still have Henry Parrish tagging along," Jonah returned.

"That we have. We wouldn't go nowhere without Henry along," Coffee replied.

Jonah sidled up to the scout's horse and shook his hand. "I've missed you, Henry."

The old scout grinned, "We'll catch up as soon as I get these sodjar boys settled."

Before the day was over, Major General William Carroll arrived with three thousand Tennessee militiamen and eleven hundred federal muskets.

"It just might be that we now have the men and supplies to defend the city," Jonah admitted to Ana that afternoon.

It was December 21, and Jackson was very concerned, knowing that the British had to be close. "They'll be in the city before we know it," he said to Captain Reid.

A detachment of the third regiment of militia was sent to scout along the outlying waterways between the city, a bend in the Mississippi River known as English Turn, and Lake Borgne. Major Gabriel Villere, who was the son of General Jacques Villere, was in command.

As the party made ready to leave, Gabriel spotted Jonah and called to him, "Care to come along for an outing, M'sieur."

"Why not," Jonah replied. He and Moses were starting to grow weary of not having some function to keep them busy.

Ana had met a nice lady, who was a widow, named Mrs. Cindy Veigh. They were meeting with several other women to make bandages for the upcoming battle. If, in fact, a battle would take place. It was almost Christmas, and not a Redcoat had been seen. Probably turned back to Mobile, some said, and this was indeed a fear eating at Jackson.

As the party rode out of town, Jonah, riding the mule, noticed the major had a sergeant, eight white men, and three Negroes in his party. It wasn't long before the group had made it to the Villere's plantation and so far they'd not spotted anything that even looked suspicious.

Speaking to Jonah, Major Villere said, "The last thing I want is to miss an invading army making ready to attack the city without Jackson knowing it."

"Agreed," Jonah said.

The major continued, "There's a small Spanish fishing village on the left bank of Bayou Bienvenue, about a mile and a half from Lake Borgne. I think I'll send Sergeant Ducros down that way to see if there is any sign.

PART III

Old Hickory said, "We could take 'em by surprise
If we didn't fire our muskets till we looked 'em in the eyes
We held our fire till we seed their faces well
Then we opened up our squirrel gun and gave 'em well.

We fired our guns and the British kept a comin'
There wasn't nigh as many as there was a while ago
We fired once more and they began to runnin'
On down the Mississippi to the Gulf of Mexico.

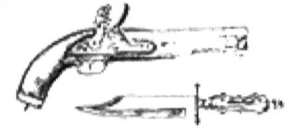

CHAPTER FIFTEEN

It was mid-morning and Major Villere was worried. "They should have been back by now, Jonah. It doesn't take this long to get there and back."

"Might be that they've spotted the British, and they're trying to get an accurate report together," Moses said.

Jonah felt uneasy. "I think I'll look around."

"I better stay here," Villere said. "You two don't get far out of sight. It's easy to get lost in that swamp."

Moses and Jonah smiled, as they walked off, leading Moses' horse and Coco and tying them to a tree. They had grown up in the swamps. The two had just got in the tree line when Moses hissed, "Down, Jonah." The two men had been together a long time and knew each other's ways well. Jonah dropped down beside Moses, who was pointing to the south. Redcoats...Redcoats, and not just a few of them, with more coming out of the swamp. The Villere's house was basically surrounded. Quietly, Jonah and Moses moved until they could see the front of Villere's house. They were in time to see Major Villere with his hands in the air, taken into his home.

"What do we do now," Jonah thought aloud.

"First thing is to see how many there are of them," Moses said. "You scout about but don't get caught."

As his friend started to ease off, Jonah called to him, "Moses!" When his friend turned, Jonah whispered, "You get caught, you act like you are a slave. I doubt that they'll even hold you if you are a house servant for the Villere's. If they ask about your rifle, tell them you're hunting a gator so they can have gator tail for dinner tonight."

Moses smiled, "I know how to get by. You're the one who has to keep out of sight."

Jonah watched Moses until he was out of sight. "Don't take any chances," he whispered, "don't take any chances." Moving so that he could get a view of the back of the house, Jonah was in time to see Villere jump out of a window. He landed hard on the ground. The sound caused people to look around. Spying their prisoner fleeing, the British started firing. Jonah started to return fire but realized one ball would be of little benefit. *My best bet is to angle through the swamp and meet up with the major,* he decided. Taking time to get the mule, he was about fifty yards behind when Villere made it to the tree line. Splinters stung the major's face as a musket ball tore into a cypress tree where he paused to catch his breath. Jonah was now close enough that Major Villere could see him.

"Go," Jonah shouted. "I'll follow."

Villere undoubtedly knew the area better than Jonah. However, the British were coming fast. To make matters worse, the major's dog was following, barking, and leading the Redcoats to them. They were now deep into the swamp and couldn't see the British. But the dog must have thought it a game as he kept jumping up on his master and barking. A shout from the British let them know that they'd been spotted, and then a shot followed.

"Go home, boy," Villere scolded the dog. He walked off a few feet, but when Jonah and Major Villere took off again, he was right behind them again. Villere stopped so fast that Jonah almost collided with him, as he picked up a stick and threw it at the dog. The dog dodged the stick and brought it back.

"He will be the death of us, Jonah. You go on and I'll let the British catch me."

"You can't do that. You know how to reach Jackson and I don't. I could find my way but the Redcoats would be in New Orleans before I got there," Jonah replied.

"I can't kill the damn dog, Jonah. I've had him since he was a puppy," Villere said.

More firing and bark flew from the tree where Jonah was standing. They also heard a yelp; the major's dog was down.

"Damn their souls to hell. They've killed my dog," said the major as he was trying for Jonah's gun.

At least we didn't have to do it, Jonah thought. "Let's go before they get any closer." Mounting the mule, they took off.

They had not gone far when Jonah stopped Villere, "Listen, they're cutting through the swamp to our left. Somebody must be leading them."

"Probably that damn Spanish fisherman. I told father not to trust them," Villere answered.

Looking down their back trail, the British were still not in sight. "We've got to hide," Jonah said.

"Look," Villere tapped Jonah's shoulder. "If we can get in that tree we got it made."

A huge oak tree full of moss sat just off the trail. Getting off Coco, Jonah swatted him with a branch. *If I lose him, Ana will kill me*, he thought. Hurrying to the tree, the men climbed as far up as possible. They had just moved some moss around to offer more cover when the British came by.

When the Redcoats were out of sight, Jonah remarked, "They never even looked up."

After fighting the mosquitoes for an hour and seeing no more Redcoats, the men skinned down the tree. Jonah followed Major Villere to the river. Finding a pirogue, they crossed the river. They soon met up with Colonel Denis de la Ronde. The colonel, like Major Villere, had been captured and escaped. The three men soon came upon a group of slaves. The slaves belonged to Mr. Dussan de la Croix. They headed to de la Croix's house. Once there, horses were furnished to the three men.

Taking the horses, they all galloped back to New Orleans. On the outskirts of the city, Jonah pulled up. "You go tell the General. I will go inform my fiancé and change. I also want to see if Moses made it back. I'll change," he added looking at his clothes, "and meet you at headquarters." The men agreed and took off.

Jonah had just walked in the door when Ana rushed up. "You've been gone over a day. I was so worried about you, when Coco came back without you." She then stepped back and looked at her man. Seeing his mud crusted and stained clothing, she said, "There's trouble."

Shaking his head yes, Jonah said, "The Redcoats are here."

Ana's hand went to her mouth, "You'll be leaving."

"But not for long," Jonah replied quickly. "If we don't hurry though, they may be sharing our breakfast."

"That close?" Ana asked.

"I'm afraid so." Jonah was removing his clothes as he spoke. "I need a quick bath and a change of clothes. Then..."

"Then can wait," Ana said. She called a servant to fill up the bathtub. As soon as hot water was brought in, she took off her clothes and bathed her man. With their bodies still damp, she then led him to the bed. "You'll not leave me without making love to me, Jonah Lee."

JACKSON HAD JUST SIGNED and sealed a letter to his wife, Rachel. He'd ended the letter 'all's well.' There was a commotion as horses thundered up to the headquarters. People, up and down Royal Street, were looking out their windows at the men pushing their horses thus. Walking to the window, Jackson felt an unexplained shiver.

The duty officer knocked on Jackson's door, announcing the three men who had arrived with urgent news. The officer was then fairly brushed aside and the three men stood there before the general.

Muddy, stained and out of breath, de la Croix nearly shouted, "The British! They've arrived. They are encamped at the Villere's plantation, not nine miles from the city."

The general allowed Major Villere to relate his story. When the major finished his narrative, the general raised his bowed body erect, to its full height. With fire in his eyes, he slammed his fist down with a terrible blow on his table. "By the Eternal, they shall not sleep on our soil." Turning to an aide, the general ordered a glass of wine to refresh his visitors.

By this time, all the secretaries and aides had filled the room. The perception of a smile was noted, as the general looking up from his glass of wine spoke, "Gentlemen, the British are below. We must fight them tonight. I will smash them."

BY THE TIME JONAH got to the headquarters, several commanding officers were showing up. Captain Reid was handing a man orders for Commodore Patterson. Jackson was sending the fourteen-gun schooner down the river. The *USS Carolina* would be their artillery.

"You have been on board ship during battle, Jonah," Reid said. "You want to go aboard the *Carolina*?"

"I think not," Jonah replied. He then asked, "Have you seen Moses?"

Reid answered, "No, I surely haven't?"

Jonah couldn't help but feel sick. Seeing Captain Lieupo, Jonah approached him with the same question.

"No, I'm sorry, but the last time I saw him was at dinner the other evening," Lieupo said.

Jackson, seeing Jonah alongside Lieupo, called to him. "As I recall, you and Captain Lieupo made a name for yourselves as trusted scouts at Horseshoe Bend."

"Yes, sir."

"Could you put together a scouting party and reconnoiter the area? I'd like to know if there's been any change before we get there," Jackson said.

"Yes, sir," Jonah answered quickly. This would give him a chance to look for Moses.

"I'll go along as well," Richard Smith volunteered.

"Good," Jackson replied. "Jonah."

"Yes sir."

"Remember this is a reconnaissance mission. I do not desire you to engage the enemy," Jackson spoke strongly.

"Yes, sir," Jonah answered. He had his orders. Walking down the headquarters' steps, he spoke, "Get your horses and meet me at the hotel." Without another word, he swung up on his horse's back and headed off. He intended to pick up Donnie, Tim, and Scrap. He'd also inform Otis that Jackson was forming up his Army.

Ana was at the door to meet him when he rode into the courtyard and dismounted. "Scrap and the Halls are putting their gear together. I told them that you'd headed to the Headquarters. They were going to meet you there."

"We have been assigned as forward scouts," Jonah said. "We don't want the army to walk into a trap."

"I don't want you to either," Ana replied, taking Jonah's hand as she spoke.

Seeing the worry on his woman's face, Jonah leaned down and kissed her forehead, her nose, and then her lips. "This should not be dangerous. We are not to even engage the enemy."

Ana looked up and smiled, "Things don't always go as planned."

"They will this time or we'll have to answer to Jackson," Jonah said.

"Damn Jackson! It's me you'll have to answer to, Jonah Lee," Ana exclaimed.

Surprised at Ana's outburst, Jonah couldn't help but smile. "You are so pretty when you get angry."

"I mean it, Jonah. You get killed and I'll never forgive you."

"Ana, sweetheart, don't worry. I'll get back to you, that's a promise."

Ana whispered, with her head hung down, "You better, Jonah, you better."

After kissing her on the head and giving her a squeeze, Jonah asked, "Is Otis here?"

"No, some man rode up and told him to form up his militia."

"Good," Jonah replied.

Their conversation was then interrupted as Scrap, Tim, and Donnie walked out from the stables, with their horses saddled and their guns in hand.

"Where we be off to?" Scrap asked.

Jonah answered him saying, "To do a little scouting as soon as Richard Smith and Captain Lieupo get here."

"That's them now," Tim said, pointing with his long rifle.

"That's all thar be of us?" Scrap inquired.

"We are just scouting, not starting the war."

"Didn't figure we was, lessen we had 'nother three or four men," Scrap replied.

"I kin tell that he ain't from Kentucky," Donnie said. "Were he, he'd have said we got one or two too many."

"Hush up," Scrap hissed, but smiled like everybody else was doing.

Lieupo looked at Jonah and said, "Well, don't just keep standing there, Jonah. Kiss the girl and let's be off. We need to be there before Coffee is."

"Now you hush up, Captain Lieupo," Smith said. "We'll just mosey out and you catch up, Jonah."

"Thanks, Richard, but that won't be necessary." Giving Ana a quick smack on the lips, Jonah turned away and, mounting his horse, led the scouting party off.

"SEE YOU DIDN'T BRING that blame mule," Donnie volunteered.

"I thought I'd lost him earlier. I'd not chance it again," Jonah replied.

"No, me neither," Smith said. "Not if you want to keep your woman."

The six men rode at a steady clip for nearly six miles. They then slowed to a walk and split up with three riders on each side of the road. They had not ridden very much further when they came upon a slave tacking papers to a tree.

"Hand me one of those," Jonah ordered. After reading the paper, he swore, "It's a proclamation."

He then handed it to Captain Lieupo, who read it to the rest of the group.

A Proclamation

Louisianians! Remain quiet and in your houses, your slaves shall be preserved to you and your property will be respected. We make war only against Americans.

Signed by

Admiral Cochrane   Major General Keane

"A bit cheeky, I'd say," Richard Smith volunteered.

"What does it say below that?" Donnie asked.

"Same thing, I expect," Lieupo answered. "It appears to be written in both French and Spanish."

Looking at the paper, Tim mused, "Nary a word of American. It's like Richard said, a cheeky bunch if you ask me."

Looking down at the slave, Jonah asked, "Whose plantation is that?"

"Mr. de la Ronde, and just beyond that is the Lacoste's plantation."

"Are the British at either of those plantations?" Jonah inquired.

"No, suh, they weren't there when I set out. They still at General Villere's place. Camped all over the yard, they were and sum down by the river too."

"How many would you say?" Captain Lieupo asked.

"I don't rightly know, but it's a heap of 'em. Hardly room to walk in places."

"All right," Jonah said. "You know the way to New Orleans, don't you?"

"Yes, suh!"

"You head that way then, and don't you come back today."

"Yes, suh!"

"Go and don't come back," Jonah repeated to the boy.

"No, suh, I won't. Not today."

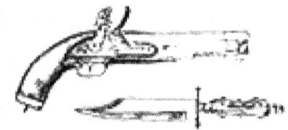

CHAPTER SIXTEEN

THE SCOUTS CONTINUED ON horseback until the boundary between the la Ronde and Lacoste plantations was visible. Leaving their horses tied to a tree just inside the wood line, they approached the Lacoste plantation house on foot. At the back of the house were several huts or slave quarters.

Seeing a male slave, Jonah called to him, "Are you the overseer?"

"No, suh, he's in that first house."

"Go fetch him," Jonah ordered. The overseer came out of the house and approached Jonah.

"Where is everybody?" Jonah asked.

"All gone, sir."

"Are any of the Redcoats about?" Jonah inquired.

"No, sir. There are none here, but there are some at the Villere's place," the overseer replied.

"How many slaves are here?" Jonah asked.

"About twenty-five close by, sir. Them's house and garden slaves and stable slaves."

Jonah nodded and said, "There's going to be a battle here soon. Round up all of your people and go over to Mr. la Ronde's place, so you'll be out of the line of fire. If anybody asks you why you left, you tell them that Mr. Jonah Lee told you to. You got that?"

"Mr. Jonah Lee, yes, sir. Mr. Jonah Lee," the overseer said.

"That was thoughtful of you," Smith said as they moved on.

"It's not their war," Jonah replied.

As the men made it to the back of Lacoste's house, they peered around. There in the distance was the Villere's house, and around it was a sea of red.

"My God, the Redcoats," Smith hissed.

"Don't know how many but it's a thousand, at least," Lieupo said.

"We need to know how many. Let me climb up that tree," Tim volunteered.

A tall oak tree was just off the front corner of the house. Tim squatted down and bolted toward the tree, keeping low to the ground. Once there, he jumped up and caught a low limb and climbed up the tree. After a few minutes, he came down and ran back to the others. "There's, at least, a thousand on this side of the house and two field pieces. I can see Redcoats all the way to the river. I'd say that they're no more than two hundred yards from here, and they've got pickets within one hundred fifty yards from us."

"There's only one thing left to do. We've got to see what's on the other side of the house," Jonah said.

"We'll have to go back a ways," Tim replied. "It's too open to try it any other way."

As the men got back behind the house and to the line of trees, Jonah paused, "Scrap, you go back and meet the general. Tell him what we've found out so far, and let him know we're trying to check out the other side of the house. We'll catch up as soon as we can." Without a word, Scrap mounted his horse and took off.

Once he was away, Donnie looked at Jonah, "You looking to count Redcoats or are you looking fer Moses?"

Jonah didn't speak for a moment, having been taken aback by the question. "Both, I reckon."

"That's what I thought. Tim and I will go down by the river and see if there's any sign of him. You three go look and see how many of the enemy they be," Donnie said.

Donnie and Tim worked their way back to a narrow wood line that made its way to the levee that held the Mississippi back.

"If this levee was to break, a lot of people would lose all they had," Tim mused as the two men worked their way silently to where they could see the British encampment.

After watching a while, it was apparent numerous slaves walked about freely, apparently seeing to the needs of the British soldiers. Some of them were carrying water, while others had a fire going and appeared to be cooking. By the cook fire, a black man stood more erect and seemed to be taking in all that was going on.

"What are you looking at?" a Redcoat sergeant demanded.

It was Moses. "Just making shore you sojer men are being taken care of," he replied. "Most dem boys ain't nothin' but field hands. They don't know nothin' bout caring foh folks."

"So you're a bloody house slave?"

"Yes, suh...just like my papa and mama."

"Do you want to be freed?" the sergeant asked.

"Oh yes, suh, I sho' does," Moses replied.

"Stick with us and I'll see if I can't get you a job with an officer. He could get you in the army."

"Thank ya, suh. Would I get to wear one of dem red sojer suits?"

"Sure you would." With that being said, the sergeant turned and left.

Once the sergeant was out of sight, Moses bent over the fire. Suddenly, he rose up and listened, a bird call...only it wasn't a known bird. It was one of his people. Turning to a soldier who'd walked up, Moses said, "I put out some 'set lines' down at the river. I'm going to go check 'em out. Might be, we has us'n some catfish stew. Mmm, talk about good."

"Do you need some help?" the soldier asked.

"Naw, suh. Jus' let me get that big ole pot yonder to put my catch in," Moses said.

The soldier actually picked up a pot and handed it to Moses. "So it's good, is it?"

"Lawd, my mouth is watering, just thinkin' on it."

"Well, hurry back then. You've got my stomach talking to me now."

"Yes, suh. It shouldn't take no more than an hour; maybe less if all dem hooks got a fish." Nodding, the Redcoat turned away.

Once over the levee, Moses turned and ran up river a hundred yards or so, and then climbed up the levee. Donnie and Tim were there grinning at their friend. Moses looked at them and asked, "What are you two doing?"

"Looking for you," Donnie replied.

Moses nodded his head and then said, "Is Jonah with you?"

"He's looking on the other side," Tim said.

Nodding again, Moses said, "In case we get separated, the British have over two thousand soldiers already landed with a brace of field guns and more are coming. Should we get caught, I'm going to say that you took me. They will believe that but if we see the British, both of you take off if you can. I'll try to slow them down."

Without another word being said, the three took off and were waiting behind Lacoste's house when Jonah, Lieupo, and Richard Smith returned.

"See you decided to show up," Moses quipped.

Jonah smiled, "We have been checking shacks to see if you'd taken advantage of some girl."

"No, but I learned a lot about those Redcoats."

"Good," Jonah said, putting his arm around Moses. "I'd hate to think you'd been idle." Both men smiled, they were together again.

The sun was starting to sink and Jonah was sure Jackson's forces would be arriving soon. They needed to go meet him with their scouting report.

Leaving Scrap to watch for any changes, the rest of the scouting party headed back down the road towards New Orleans. They had ridden to within four miles of the city when they heard the sound of horses.

"Has to be the army," Smith volunteered.

The others agreed, but for safety's sake they pulled into the wood line on each side of the road.

"Damn swampy," Smith hissed. "Any further and our horses would sink up to their belly."

When it was obvious that it was Jackson's army, the scouts pulled into the road. Without thinking about it, Jonah gave a salute, which Jackson returned in a professional manner. Riding beside the general, Jonah recognized the LaFitte brothers, as well as General Coffee, and Colonel Thomas Hinds with his Light Dragoons. Next to Coffee sat Jonah's friend, Henry Parrish.

General Jackson looked at Jonah and asked, "Any more news on our enemy?"

"As near as we can figure, General, there's about two thousand British camped in and around the Villere home. There are at least two and maybe three field pieces."

"Hmm! Sir," interrupted Moses. "I overheard a conversation where a junior officer asked the apparent commander, General John Keane, why they didn't push on. If they did they could be at the city's door in no time. 'Major,' Keane had replied, 'We have no horses. Only a few pieces of light artillery and no supplies, whereas Jackson has strength of some twenty thousand men.' 'I see, sir,' the major said and walked away."

"Our misinformation has served its purpose," Jackson said. "Let's be off before we're discovered."

It was nearly six o'clock when Jackson began maneuvering part of his command to flank the British. Jonah asked for and was given permission to join General Coffee. Jackson sent Coffee's men, including a group of New Orleans sharpshooters under Captain Thomas Beale, and the Mississippi dragoons, in a circuitous route to the edge of the swamp behind de la Ronde's place, where they might be able to charge and push the British into the river. Having already followed this route searching for Moses, Donnie and Tim led the way.

In the growing darkness, Jackson spread his remaining soldiers near the river. The marines and artillery, along with the balance of the Seventh and Forty-Fourth, were spread along the levee road. As the light continued to fade, Jonah, Moses, Scrap, and the Halls quietly advanced with Coffee's riflemen. Captain Lieupo and Richard Smith would serve as messengers to Jackson.

Along the river, two schooners crewed mostly by ninety of LaFitte's men and the *Carolina* commanded by Commodore Patterson reached their position opposite the British camp.

"Don't see why them Redcoats ain't shooting at the gunboats," Scrap whispered. "They got to see 'em."

"Probably thinks they're gunboats from Admiral Cochrane," Jonah replied.

"They'll be in for a surprise soon then," Donnie threw out.

"Its 7:30," Tim volunteered. His words were punctuated as the gunboats opened up.

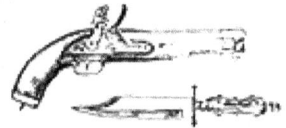

CHAPTER SEVENTEEN

THE SURPRISE WAS BETTER than Jackson could have hoped for. The British soldiers had been led to believe the Americans would have little support once the Redcoats showed up. They quickly learned their error. Flames spewed forth, lighting up the night, as the *Carolina* and two smaller gunboats let loose their cannons filled with grape shot upon the British encampment. The peaceful camp was suddenly a mass of confusion and death. Officers tried to restore their troops as the schooner and gunboats continued their thunderous barrage. Men tried to put out campfires to cut down on the visibility of their camps. Their efforts were futile. One of the officers tried to bring their artillery to bear and went so far as to launch rockets. Someone even rounded up enough men to fire squad after squad of musket fire. Yet all of this proved ineffective.

Jonah sat on his mount with Moses, Scrap and the Halls around him. All had seen land battles with each side firing artillery. But only Jonah, of all of General Coffee's men, had firsthand experience in regards to a naval battle. This was totally different. A naval bombardment on shore-based soldiers when there'd been no expectation was something new. No fortification to give any means of relief...any amount of protection. It was both amazing and gut wrenching at the same time. It was, in fact, a living hell...hell on earth. Something no one could put words to. Men started to withdraw to the woods where the trees gave some degree of cover, while others rushed to the levee where the naval fire could not be depressed enough to fire on them.

After thirty minutes of raining death upon the encampment, the guns ceased firing as Jackson had ordered Commodore Patterson. A red, white, and blue trail of rockets lit up the night sky, signaling Jackson's units to the west to start moving forward along the path of the Mississippi River. These units were made up of the Seventh and Forty-fourth Infantry Regiment. As the river curved, the men were pushed more inland, approaching the still flickering campfires. Jackson brought his forces into line and directed the charge. He ordered his artillery, two six-pounders, to open up. Watching this, Jonah and the men under General Coffee were itching to join the fight. Yet Coffee, Jackson's strong right hand, had his men to sit tight in their saddles. The horses were stamping and pawing, shaking their hands and blowing. These were war horses and they were as eager as the men to get into the action. After several rounds from the six pounders were fired, the British put together a group of men to take them. Watching the British charge, Jonah felt apprehensive. When it looked like the British would gain the upper hand, troops from the Seventh Infantry responded, beating back the British charge and saving the guns. Still no orders were given to charge.

Scrap reached into his pocket and took a bite from a twist of tobacco he was carrying. He offered a chew to those close by, but had no takers. The Seventh had finished its sudden fierce melee with the Redcoats, when orders came for the men to push forward. Soon after making initial contact with the British, the Redcoats were routed from behind a thick hedge row and a wide ditch. Someone on the *Carolina* had a night glass and saw the Redcoats retreat. Patterson gave the order and once again the ship's guns opened up and began to rake the British troops. Even in the dark, Jonah's group watched as muzzle flashes lit up the night and they could see men fall to the deadly grape.

Richard Smith rode up in a gallop. He saluted General Coffee and had to shout to be heard above the gunfire. "General Jackson's compliments, sir, you may charge when it is convenient."

"Hear that, Scrap?" Moses asked. "You better spit before you get a belly full of chaw."

Scrap grinned and spit a stream of juice, but didn't spit out the tobacco. Tim Hall, who was looking at them, just shook his head.

"You heard the man," General Coffee yelled. "At the forward... charge."

The men let out with a wild yell and restless horses surged forward. They were at the enemy quickly. Pistols were fired and then it was the blades. The Redcoats were being hacked down by sabers, tomahawks, and huge hunting knives. At first, there was a struggle as the opposition tried to repulse the charge. Jonah felt himself being pulled from the saddle, but a vicious swing from Richard Smith severed the Redcoat's arm. Blood was still dripping from Smith's tomahawk as he smiled and rode on.

The British got off a few musket shots, creating flashes, but few found their mark. Soon the resistance melted and the enemy ran. Coffee's brigade continued to push hard and swiftly. They were soon so far forward that they were within a thousand yards of Jackson's command, near the edge of the woods where the swamp began. The movement had happened so fast that numerous British began to surrender. As Coffee's men continued to flank the British, they soon captured both the commanding officers of Britain's Ninety-fifth Rifles and fifty Redcoat soldiers.

About eleven p.m., Coffee's men were now in danger of being outflanked. He left the field of battle, men and horses were thoroughly worn out. As they left, they could see the British had circled in the dark and now were closing next to the Villere's plantation house.

General Carroll had now arrived with his Tennesseans. A quick officer's call was made. Jonah, as the president's man, stood to the side and listened as Carroll argued to push forward and end it now. But this was not an open battlefield. Men were scattered in the woods, the swamp, along the levee, and around Villere's house. There had already been a few instances of friend firing on friend. Besides, what was to keep the British from leaving enough men as a decoy and then attacking New Orleans. Jackson had made up his mind, and it was doubtful that he'd change it. It made good sense to Jonah. Jackson had not driven the British from American soil, but he had stopped their advance and showed them that it would not be a pleasant journey to the city, if they made it that far.

Seeing Jonah, Jackson asked, "What do you say, Jonah?"

"I agree with you, General. We've given them what for. We've also put them on notice. They will now have to stop, add up their losses and decide on a plan. I think that we should put out pickets but retire for the night. We have a few wounds to lick ourselves. We need powder, shot, food, and water. I'd hate to come up short when we've just won a major round." Jonah paused. Everyone was looking at him, and some were stunned. He realized that he'd been asked if he agreed, and that was only out of courtesy. He'd not been asked to deliver a sermon. Swallowing, he smiled and said, "Yes sir, I agree with you, General."

"Glad to hear it," Jackson said, and now everyone was smiling.

The captain gave Jonah a gentle slap on the back. "Damn, Jonah that was a mouthful."

"As if anybody cared," replied Jonah.

Reid then stopped as he'd started to walk on, "Oh, some care, Jonah, a few do but one in particular."

Soon shots were heard from the direction of Villere's house. Henry Parrish rode up and reported to General Coffee, but everybody heard. "The British have reinforcements coming up. They sent out skirmishers but we sent them packing. That was the shots that you heard. We caught hold of one of 'em and he's whistling up a storm. Seems their general is a man named Keane. Them's that coming 'pears to be more of the Ninety-fifth. I hear there's to be an attempt for our boats."

"Thank you, Henry."

"Do you want to question them soldiers we took any further, General Coffee?" Henry asked.

"Yes, let Captain Reid talk to him. If he can't get anything from him, maybe one of our Indian brothers will loosen his tongue."

As Reid left, a man named John Macarty was introduced to Jackson. Mr. Macarty had come to offer his house as General Jackson's battlefield headquarters. Jackson graciously accepted and a group followed the man back to his home.

"Well, Jonah, it has been a very busy night," General Coffee said. "By the morrow, we should know the measure." By that, he meant how many men had been killed, wounded, or missing. Hopefully, it would be to their benefit.

Captain Lieupo walked up. "We've been ordered to camp at the de la Ronde plantation, Jonah. You are welcome to camp with us but if you want to return to New Orleans, we've got men taking some wounded back for treatment. They're to return at first light, but you are, of course, free to return as you wish."

When Jonah seemed to be pondering his decision, Coffee added, "Were it me, I would go take a bath and sleep in a comfortable bed."

"I agree with you," Jonah said. "I think the British will regroup before they attack."

"So go home. When the real fighting starts, you may not get a chance."

Jonah went over to his group. Scrap decided to stay, but Moses, Donnie, and Tim all decided to ride back with Jonah.

Captain Lieupo walked up as they mounted their horses. "I'll ride back with you men. The general has a list of things for me to check on and orders to deliver."

"Where's Richard Smith?" Jonah asked.

"Running orders over to Patterson, last I seen." Without another word, Lieupo mounted up and the men rode the nine miles back to New Orleans.

Jonah went in the back door to their suite. Ana heard the horses as they rode into the courtyard. Jonah now totally exhausted allowed her to give him a quick sponge off as he gave a summary of the battle.

"I was so worried, Jonah. I'm so glad you came home. Will you be able to come home every night, Jonah...Jonah?"

But there was no reply as Jonah had lain back across the bed while Ana tugged at his boots, he was asleep, dead to the world. Ana pulled his legs up more on the bed and then, blowing out the lantern, she crawled into the bed beside him. He may be sound asleep, but he was back...back safe and sound, and lying next to her. Snuggling closer, she whispered a prayer and closed her eyes. Her man was back. He'd be leaving again in the morning, but for now he was back and she felt safe. Tomorrow was another day.

CHAPTER EIGHTEEN

THE CROWING ROOSTER WOKE Jonah. Ana was already dressed as he sat up in bed. "Richard Smith is in the dining room," she said.

Jonah got up, walked over to Ana and kissed her good morning. "That was worth the ride home last night," he said.

Smiling, Ana said, "You better hurry if you want any breakfast."

"I'll tell you what I'd rather have."

"Oh, Jonah, it would be nice but you need to eat if you're going back with Smith," Ana replied.

"With Smith, who said?"

"I do," Ana said, and quickly stepped out of the room before he changed her mind.

Jonah was soon dressed and sat down next to Richard Smith and Steve Lieupo. "No war to fight today?" he asked, as he took the cup of coffee Ana poured for him.

"None so far," Smith answered. "It doesn't appear the British is in any hurry this morning. Jackson was up at the break of day and surveying the land. He's decided to dig in right where he is. There's a drainage ditch between Villere's and de la Ronde's properties that extends from the main road alongside the dike to deep within that big cypress swamp. He sent a detail into the city to get one thousand picks and shovels. Slaves from the surrounding plantations have been put to work widening and deepening the ditch. They are using the dirt to form a parapet running the entire length from the dike to the swamp. He's sent General Coffee's Choctaw Indians into the swamp to keep watch in case the Redcoats try to sneak some units in that way."

Jonah looked at Smith and said, "I'm surprised the British are allowing us the time to build up defenses."

"Jackson put the word out if anybody was captured and questioned about our strength, they were to say we had twenty thousand men and ten thousand reinforcements had just arrived in New Orleans. That number would make any British commander stop and reassess his plans."

"I'm sure last night's attack killed their notion that taking the city would be an easy conquest," Steve Lieupo said, joining in after taking the last bite of a buttered biscuit smeared with a generous portion of honey. He looked at his empty cup and stood up to get the coffee pot but a waiter quickly got the pot and filled his cup.

Pausing a second to see if Ana was close by, Jonah asked, "What was the butcher's bill?"

Smith answered, "Better than I expected, with everybody shooting at anything that moved in the dark. We had twenty-four killed, about one hundred fifteen wounded, and seventy-four missing as far as we can tell. We figure the British had double our twenty-four killed, and over one hundred fifty wounded. One of Coffee's captains said that several British officers were killed trying to rally the troops."

"I saw some of them fall," Jonah admitted. What he didn't say was he knew one had fallen to his blade.

"The next one won't be a quick battle like it was last night," Smith threw out. "Scrap and a few others went out last night and watched as boatload after boatload of reinforcements come ashore. Scrap even heard two officers discussing how Admiral Cochrane and General Pakenham had gotten into a heated argument about how to take the city. Cochrane felt it best to continue as it was, saying his boats could supply every need while the general wanted to take the Chef Menteur Road to invade the city."

"Sounds like the admiral has won out for now." Jonah replied.

Across the dining room, two merchants walked in and sat down. "He has gone too far," the one man grumbled to his friend. "Seizing cotton bales to add to the defense."

The other man was smiling at his friend, "Well, Charles, the captain was right. The price of cotton is down and if the Redcoats take the city, they will take it. So just look on the bright side. Your cotton may help in the keeping of your warehouses, if Jackson can beat the British."

Jonah, Smith, and Lieupo all smiled but didn't say a word. *You got to give it to Jackson*, Jonah thought. *The man knows how to improvise.* After breakfast, Richard Smith and Captain Lieupo rode back to the lines.

Jonah saw Donnie and Tim, "Have you had breakfast?"

"Lord, yeah, hours ago," Donnie replied.

"I just finished mine. Smith says Jackson is building an earthwork, so unless you want to get on the business end of a pick or shovel, I wouldn't be in any rush."

"Wonder why the British hasn't attacked," Donnie mused.

"Trying to regroup and form another plan," Jonah said. He then added, "But that's a huge error on their part. Gives Jackson time to dig in and they'll play hell, rooting him out."

"That's what we figured," Tim responded. He then smiled as Moses entered from the kitchen.

Moses was eating a biscuit that was cut in half, with a link of sausage put between the two halves. "Any coffee left?" he asked.

By the time Jonah, Moses, and the Halls made it to Jackson's army, they were totally surprised. Jackson had retreated back from the Villere's plantation about two miles to the Rodriguez Canal. The men had dug out the ditch and made a rampart six hundred yards or so long. Jackson was on his horse going up and down the earthwork.

"He's seldom been off that horse all day," Henry Parrish volunteered as he rode up. "He's got more cussedness and determination than any man I know." After a brief catching up, Henry said, "I gotta go see if them Choctaws need anything."

"Are they still in the swamp?" Moses asked.

"Yep, what better place is they? They're right at home amongst them cottonmouths, gators, and such."

The men smiled at the old scout. He'd be just as at home, Jonah figured. The night was coming on and after lending a hand here and there, as well as running errands for Jackson, Jonah decided there was little reason to stay around. They'd just started to head back to town when Captain Reid told them Jackson planned to work through the night if need be. But he'd like to know if there was any change in the British camp. The meaning of this was that Jackson wanted Jonah and his friends to scout out the Redcoat camp. *Damn, so much for clean sheets and Ana's warm body*, thought Jonah. Turning as he rode away, he caught Reid smiling.

"Ruined your plans for tonight, did he?" Reid asked, with a laugh.

Seeing Jonah's gesture, Moses put his hand to his mouth in mock awe.

"Jonah," Moses chided, "that response was most ungentlemanly. I'm sure glad Mama Lee didn't see it. Of course, was she to hear about it, it'd be the same as if she saw it."

"And who's going to tell?" Jonah snarled.

Shaking his head, Moses replied, "One never knows, do they?"

Jonah made the same gesture to Moses.

"Digging that hole deeper, aren't you? I can see Mama Lee now. 'Jonah, I'm disgraced. You weren't raised that way, acting like trashy folks. What am I to do with you, boy?'"

"Moses!"

"Yeah!"

"Would you just hush?"

"I don't know. I might, and then again, I might not."

Turning to Donnie and Tim, Jonah said, "Let's ride. He isn't funny."

The men split into two groups. Within an hour, they met back up at the rendezvous area they'd decided on. Comparing notes, they headed back to Jackson's headquarters. Jackson had several visitors when the scouting party reported. Jean LaFitte and Dominique Youx, as well as General Coffee, General Carroll, and Major Daquin, who was the white commander in charge of the two hundred and ten free men of color. Otis was an officer under Major Daquin. Seeing Jonah, Jackson interrupted the genial conversation and asked Jonah to report.

"I'd say there are now upward four thousand soldiers now camped in and around the grounds of Chalmette, sir, and more coming."

"What is this Chalmette you speak of?" General Carroll asked.

Before Jonah could reply, LaFitte spoke up, "That is the name given the community that the Villere's plantation lies in, sir. The la Ronde plantation is also of the Chalmette community."

Nodding, Carroll then asked, "How close were you able to get, Jonah? Did you hear any plans for the morrow?"

"No plans, General, but the motto given to the troops was 'beauty and booty.'" This caused all the men to laugh.

"Are they still saying that?" Jackson asked.

Now, Jonah smiled as he took a cup offered him. The smell reeked of strong spirits. He took a big gulp and then answered Jackson, "Shall we say their spirits have been dampened a bit, General."

"Have they brought any added artillery?" Dominique Youx asked.

"I did not see any heavy stuff but they towed in a boatload of those rockets."

Youx snarled at this. "If they intend for those things to win the day for them, they need to think again. They do sound fearsome," Dominique added, "so the men need to be warned about the noise."

Jonah waited a beat and then added, "The British are awed by the river level being higher than the surrounding land."

"Yes, and I plan to use the river to impede the British attack," Jackson said. "But that's for the morrow."

Jonah bid the men goodnight. It was Christmas Eve. *The devil with the hour, I'm going to see Ana*, he thought. After Jackson had moved his line back, it was now just over six miles back to town. As he searched for Moses, he saw men carrying sections of fence into the camp. Leave it to Jackson to use anything at hand to help with the fortifications.

Moses was at the horses smoking a pipe. "Tim and Donnie are going to camp out here tonight."

"Tired, are they?" Jonah inquired.

"I think it had more to do with cards and corn than being tired," Moses said.

"Corn?" Jonah asked.

Moses corrected himself, "Corn squeezing." Involuntarily, Moses gave a shiver.

"You get into the corn?" Jonah asked.

"No, I think the weather is about to turn. Cold and rain, I'd guess, the way my bones feel."

"It will be hell on the troops," Jonah thought aloud.

"There is more than ours. Our men are starting to bunk up in slave's quarters," Moses replied.

Jonah looked at Moses and asked, "Where are the slaves?"

"Most of them moved over to another plantation. Some have taken the opportunity to run, I imagine," Moses answered.

"It will be hell if they get caught," Jonah replied.

"That's true, but if they are going to run, now is the time."

"Moses."

"Yeah."

"If you were a slave, would you run?"

Moses pulled back on his horse's reins and looked at his adopted brother. "I've thought about that a lot, Jonah, more so since we have been here, in New Orleans. The way I...we was raised with Mama Lee and the Colonel's teachings, it's hard to think of life as anything but free. Also being raised free, I've taken no sass off anybody like the free blacks in the city do. Otis says that it's the poor white that tries to lord over the blacks, not the men of means. If I'd been born and raised a slave, who knows how I'd feel. I might feel inferior. Not everybody believes like Mama Lee, that we're all God's children."

Jonah smiled at this and the two repeated together, "Brothers in Christ."

"I will tell you one thing though, Jonah. A black has it better than an Indian."

"You're both," Jonah said without thinking.

"Yeah, yeah I am. There have been times back in Alabama, when I have seen some of the men eyeing me. It wasn't because of the black part. It was the Indian part that scared them. They never knew when I might revert back to being a savage. They were fearful."

"They weren't afraid," Jonah said, with a snicker. "You're so damn ugly, they were afraid it would rub off." Saying this, he dug his heels into his horse and took off. Moses called out a couple of rather foul words. Hearing these, Jonah pulled up. "Now who is going to tell Mama Lee what?"

Moses cuffed him one, knocking off Jonah's hat as he rode by. Jonah leaned way over and, grasping a handful of horse's mane, he reached down and got his hat. Kicking his horse into a trot, he soon caught up to Moses. Together, the two rode into New Orleans and to the hotel.

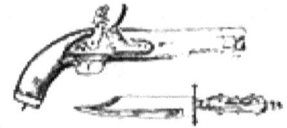

CHAPTER NINETEEN

It was Christmas Day, 1814. The Hotel Provincial's cook had outdone herself. The hotel guests had a feast to remember. Otis was away, on the lines with the rest of his regiment, but Mademoiselle Renee proved to be the perfect hostess. A buffet was set up with different breakfast meats: bacon, sausage, sugar cured ham, and a salty country ham. There were platters with buttered biscuits, honey glazed muffins, and sugary beignets. Hominy grits and oatmeal half-filled two large pots. Coffee, coffee with chicory, and hot cocoa were also available. Eggs made to order were ready in no time at all. If a guest desired fresh preserves and jelly, they were made available, along with syrup and local honey.

Moses was in the kitchen talking to Sally and Fawn. When they'd come back from LaFitte's camp on Grand Terre Island, Jonah didn't know. Their men were probably with Dominique Youx and Pierre on the front line. The kitchen door to the side yard opened and Scrap and Richard Smith walked in.

"Sho' smells good," Scrap commented.

"Better than the way you smell," Smith replied.

"You been belly down in the swamp like I has, I reckon you'd smell like something worse than fancy toilet water yourself. I plan on eating out here, anyway," Scrap said. "I wouldn't want to upset a body's disposition."

It was hard not to laugh, but Scrap did reek like stale swamp water. Looking at Jonah, Scrap said, "I was gonna eat a bite and then take a bath if I could get a maid to set up a tub while I collect my possibles."

Smiling at Scrap, Smith who towered over everybody, leaned over and whispered, "I was hoping to get a bath myself. After all, it's Christmas."

"Anything happening out at the lines?" Jonah asked.

"No, a few rounds from the Redcoats' cannons to make sure we didn't sleep in. Scrap has been in the swamp like he said, and this morning he heard something being discussed with a sentry and the corporal of the guard. Scrap waited until the corporal was out of sight, and then he sticks his rifle barrel in the sentry's ear and told him not to twitch as he had a hair trigger. He got the sentry back to headquarters where he told the news. The big man for the British ain't happy with the way he's gotten bogged down. They expected to be eating dinner in New Orleans on Christmas Day, so General Keane has been relieved. Major General Sir Edward Pakenham, who's the brother-in-law to the Duke of Wellington, has been put in charge. Pakenham's second in command is General Samuel Gibbs. It's said that Pakenham criticized everything he saw. One soldier was asked, 'Why son, why haven't we taken the enemy?' The soldier looked shocked that such a question would be asked. Finally, he got his tongue and replied, 'Bullets, sir, cannonball and bullets.'" Moses and Jonah both laughed. "That's the same reaction Jackson had," Smith volunteered.

"'hit'll do it every Gawd blessed time," Scrap added between bites of biscuit and country ham.

After breakfast, Jonah and Ana went back to their suite. "Do you have to go back to the lines today, Jonah?"

"I need to make an appearance this afternoon. I'm sending a few things, a couple of hams, fresh bread, and some beignets back with Scrap. He's going back after he cleans up."

"From what Fawn said, he needed a bath," Ana said.

"He's been lying out in a swamp for days, spying on the British," Jonah said in defense of the scout.

"I wasn't being critical," Ana responded. "I…"

Before she could speak any further, Jonah kissed her. "Next year we'll be at home for Christmas. Aunt Fannie will cook a breakfast, maybe not as big, but just as good as what we had this morning."

They had been sitting on the edge of the bed. Jonah lay back and pulled Ana to him. "You won't see snow there like you're used to, but it gets chilly. We have good neighbors, some new ones who I really like. James Anthony just inherited his uncle's farm. His mother grew up near Savannah in a small community just across the South Carolina line. His father is a British admiral. Yet James sides with the Colonies... his mother's influence. On the other side of us are Eli Taylor and his wife, Debbie. They own this hotel. He's a retired...ah...sea captain."

Ana looked at Jonah, "Is that all? You seemed to be confused about Mr. Taylor."

"Captain Taylor," Jonah corrected. "You never call a ship's captain mister."

"You're smiling again, Jonah."

Taking a deep breath and exhaling, Jonah responded, "It's a poorly kept secret that Captain Taylor was once a pirate."

Ana sat up suddenly, "He was a pirate. Your friend...a pirate."

"Shh! He was a pirate, but a good one. He never bothered an American ship."

"Humph! He told you that."

"Not personally, we don't mention it," Jonah said.

"But you believe it?" Ana asked.

"Yes...yes, I do."

"Jonah, you are incredible."

"You don't know the man. I do," Jonah replied.

"Then whose ships did he take?"

"Oh, most anybodies, I imagine. But mostly British and Spanish ships."

"But no American ship," Ana snorted.

"No American."

"Jonah, does your mama and daddy believe this?"

"I don't know that it's ever been mentioned."

"Where, please tell, did you get your information?" Ana inquired.

"From Cooper Cain," Jonah replied.

"Who is Cooper Cain?"

"He was one of Captain Taylor's men, his protégé really, when I met him. They brought Debbie, now Taylor's wife, to visit Savannah. When the visit was over, Captain Taylor wanted Cooper to see more of his new country. Cooper is from England. So Moses and I brought them back to New Orleans overland. Cooper took us home in a ship. He also brought Moses and me here...actually not exactly here, but close where we could take up the hunt for you."

"I declare, Jonah, you're a friend of the President, a friend of this Colonel Richard Mentor Johnson, who had spies that were out looking for us. You're friends with General Jackson, and now I find out you have pirate friends. That's enough to make my head swim."

"You sound like Sally now," Jonah said.

Looking mischievous, Ana looked at Jonah and said, "Speaking of Sally, do you know she told me if I didn't come to my senses, she'd bed you in a heartbeat. She said you'd never have cold sheets."

"Hmm, that does add a little interest, doesn't it? She is a handsome wench."

Hitting Jonah with a pillow, Ana said, "And so is that Captain Reid."

Pulling her down on the bed, Jonah gave his woman a long passionate kiss. "We'll be doing this in our home next year."

"Next year," she whispered. "I can't wait."

DRAINED FROM PASSION AFTER a time of lovemaking, Jonah and Ana had a mid-morning nap. When they awakened, Jonah quickly dressed. There was still a spattering of hotel guests in the dining area. Jonah poured himself a cup of inky black coffee and got a beignet. As he turned, he recognized one of the guests, Michael Benton, the artist.

"May I join you, Mr. Benton?"

"Please do. And it's Mike, not Mr. Benton."

Jonah smiled, shook Benton's hand, and took a chair. "I've had the opportunity to see some of your work, Mike. You do a magnificent job. My fiancé is envious of the painting you did for Mrs. Meeks."

Mike smiled, "Carolyn was a good subject. She was very good at following my suggestions and therefore creating an image that was pleasing to paint."

Jonah, knowing Mrs. Meeks, could understand Benton's words. Lawyer Meeks had a prize of a wife. "I will come to the point, Mike. I would like for you to do a painting for me, of my wife...well soon to be wife. I mentioned this briefly when we last spoke."

"I remember," Benton replied, and then grew serious. "Sir, the reason that I'm in New Orleans," Benton explained, "was to try to get a few paintings of Jackson and even a few battlefield sketches. But between General Carroll and Captain Reid, I can't even get close to Jackson, since the day you introduced us."

Jonah's mind started working fast. "How would you like to dine with the general tonight, battle permitting?"

"You have that ability?" Mike Benton asked.

"I do."

Benton started to smile, "I believe, sir, you've made yourself a bargain."

"Good," Jonah said. "Ana is dressing to ride out to Jackson's headquarters as we speak. You two can meet and we can work out the details as we ride."

Benton smiled and then stood up. "Is this your promised, Jonah?" he asked as a lady entered the room.

Jonah turned, smiled and then stood up. "Ana, I'd like to introduce you to Mr. Michael Benton."

Ana and Benton spoke in unison, "We've met." She then added, "Mr. Benton was at the Livingston's afternoon tea just recently." Mike bowed to Ana.

"Good, you two know each other then," Jonah said.

Ana smiled again, "We've been introduced, but I'm afraid that Mr. Benton was all eyes for Miss Earles."

"Guilty," Benton replied. "The young lady has quickly stolen my heart. Hopefully, we can further our relationship after these difficulties are over."

"I do wish you the best in those endeavors," Ana replied. "She is a very pleasant and beautiful lady."

"Thank you, Ana, and I wish you and Mr. Lee the very best."

CHAPTER TWENTY

Cannon shot was heard about a mile from Jackson's line. Jonah turned to Ana and Mike Benton, "Well, not everybody is taking the day off."

Moses and Scrap, who had been trailing the small procession, pulled up by Jonah. "We will ride on ahead. If there's any trouble brewing, we will get word back to you." With that being said, the two men took off at a gallop.

"I feel strange riding in a carriage to a battlefield," Benton said.

"If you had brought a horse, he may have been borrowed," Jonah said, smiling.

"Nobody would have taken Coco," Ana injected.

"That's her pet mule," Jonah explained and then added, "Nobody's going to unhitch a horse from a carriage either. Besides, we needed the carriage to haul all the food."

Word had gotten out quickly, probably by the kitchen staff, about taking food to the army. Suddenly people were bringing over more food than could be taken on horseback. Mike Benton drove the carriage, his big frame dwarfing Ana. She tried to bring out a conversation about Miss Kitty Earles, but Benton would only smile and change the subject. Jonah, riding alongside, could hear Ana's attempts very well. Smiling to himself, he thought, *all women are the same, nosey about another's love life and always trying to play cupid.*

The three were almost at the camp when they met Moses returning. "Everything's fine. The British were just letting Jackson know they're still around." Jonah smiled but Ana wasn't smiling.

As they drew up at Jackson's headquarters, Captain Reid walked out and met them, and hurried over to Ana's side of the carriage to help her down. "Why thank you, Captain Reid, I see there are a few gallant officers around with manners." Reid was smiling ear to ear.

Jonah looked at Benton, shaking his head. "Notice that he didn't speak to us or offer to help carry anything." Benton smiled, sensing there was no animosity between the two men.

As Jonah and Benton enter the headquarters, Jackson turned and rushed over, taking some of Jonah's burden. Seeing the general, others rushed forward to help.

"There's more in the carriage," Jonah volunteered.

Jonah smiled when Jackson spoke, "Captain Reid." Nothing else was said, but Reid grabbed a guard and walked out to bring in the rest.

"How delightful to see you, Ana," Jackson said. "I see you've brought a wonderful array of foods." Sniffing, he continued, "I detect the odor of ham and yams, an appropriate fare for the occasion."

Ana did a small curtsy, "Thank you, General. We brought a friend along; he is an artist. I thought he may be able to help preserve for history your glorious defense of New Orleans and our country." That said, Ana introduced Benton to Jackson.

"I believe we've met briefly," Jackson responded, shaking Benton's hand.

Damnation, Jonah thought. Ana has already wooed Jackson favorably over to the artist. *What a little hussy*, he thought, *using her wiles on Old Hickory*. He then thought, *maybe it's the ham*.

As the two men shook hands, Jonah also noted that Mike Benton was as tall as, if not an inch or so taller than, General Jackson. After the greetings were over, extra chairs were brought out and placed around the dining table where the food had been laid out. While Jackson and the higher ranked officers gathered around the larger table, other tables were set up here and there around the room.

A chair for Ana was placed to the right of General Jackson. As she sat down, she said, "Mr. Benton, come sit by me," relegating Jonah to a chair off to the side.

"We were not expecting such a fare. As soldiers, we often find food in short supply," General Jackson said.

"It was the least we could do for such brave men," Ana replied. Jonah couldn't believe his ears. It had been his idea, not hers. Ana then said, "Actually General, it was Jonah's idea but word got out and several others provided food as well."

"My compliments," Jackson responded politely, as he cut into a slice of ham. "So you're an artist, Mr. Benton?" Jackson asked, making conversation.

Before Benton could reply, Ana spoke, "He's an exceptional artist, General, a master at his trade. You should just see some of his portraits."

When Ana paused, Benton replied, "Portraits are what creates a living but I really love the outdoors...outdoors and ships."

A loud boom was heard and then a crash outside. The sound caused Ana and Mike Benton to jump.

"Just the British trying to keep us awake," Jackson replied, touching Ana's shoulder to calm and reassure her.

Reid, who'd been left standing, leaned over to Jonah. "Henry Parrish took a British sentry prisoner this morning. He said General Keane has officially been relieved. Sir Edward Pakenham has taken over command. He's been sending out patrols but we've driven them off with ease. The sentry said if we were smart, we'd turn him loose and bugger on out of here as General Pakenham is resolved to remove our encumbrances and push forward very soon."

"So the time is nigh," Jonah replied.

"I'm afraid so, Jonah. If Pakenham is anything like Wellington, his brother-in-law, we're in for a fight."

"Maybe he's seeking the recognition that Wellington has received," Jonah said.

Nodding, Reid replied, "Jackson feels tomorrow they'll fight."

"Are we set?" Jonah asked.

Reid smiled, "Far better than we were at Horseshoe Bend. We have the men, I believe. We have an open road to New Orleans, while they have to boat in supplies."

"How many men do we have?" Jonah asked.

"Nowhere near the twenty thousand they think we have," Reid said with a smile. "Counting sixty or so marines, a hundred sailors, one thousand plus Louisiana militia, and nearly five hundred free men of color, one thousand three hundred fifty-two Tennessee militia, nine hundred eighty-six Kentucky militia, one hundred fifty Mississippi militia, plus fifty-two of Jackson's Choctaw warriors, and LaFitte's Baratarians, and the men on the ships, I'd say we have just shy of four thousand eight hundred men."

Jonah was amazed at how Reid just rattled off the numbers from memory. That was one of the reasons that he was the general's aide.

"I noticed that we're in better shape with artillery than at Horseshoe Bend," Jonah volunteered.

Reid smiled. "Jackson has never had so many guns. Many were brought in by Dominique Youx and Pierre LaFitte. We have a big thirty-two pounder gun, three twenty-four pounders, one eighteen pounder, three twelve pounders, three six pounders, and two twenty-four inch howitzers. That's in addition to the guns on the ships." Glancing around to see who might be listening, Reid leaned over and whispered, "Patterson can crow all he wants about destroying Barataria. Had LaFitte chose to fight, Patterson and his entire crew would be crab and gator meat. That was part of Livingston's argument when he talked to Jackson."

Jonah already knew this but kept his knowledge to himself, as he'd promised Jackson he'd do.

THE MEAL HAD BEEN completed. Jackson was thanking Ana for such a wonderful surprise. He'd invited Benton to return anytime. "You'll be welcome in our camp," Jackson said.

Outside a loud shriek was heard following cannonballs hitting outside in the yard. Several ran outside, including Ana. A soldier was lying on the ground almost cut in two, but still alive and crying out in pain.

Jackson turned Ana away from the scene. "I think you should take your lady home now, Jonah."

"Yes sir. I will be back before first light," Jonah replied.

Jackson nodded, turned and went back inside his headquarters. Mike Benton watched as men gathered up the poor fellow on a stretcher and ran off with him. The ride back to New Orleans was done in silence. It was only after they arrived at the Hotel Provincial that anyone spoke.

"Thank you for inviting me," Benton said. "You've kept your part of the bargain so I will keep mine and it will be a privilege."

A doorman came and took Jonah's horse, while Benton helped Ana down from the carriage. As Ana headed inside, Benton said, "I'll ride out with you in the morning." Shaking Jonah's hand, Benton turned and followed Ana inside the hotel.

Jonah started to lead the horse pulling the carriage around to the stable when the same doorman, boy actually, rushed back.

"I've got him for you, Mr. Lee." Taking hold, the boy walked off with the horse and carriage.

Dreading to face Ana, Jonah reluctantly walked in. Thus far this hadn't really been a war at all. The citizens of New Orleans went about their daily lives much the same as every other day. The war seemed distant. But would it continue to be so? Jonah didn't think so, especially if the Redcoats overrun Jackson. The war then would be felt. Hopefully, not as bad as in Washington, where the British had taken the town, ransacked it and then burned it. But that was after they had enjoyed a meal that had been laid out at the White House by the president's wife, Dolly. Thinking of how Washington was destroyed made Jonah shiver.

Taking a deep breath and exhaling with a sigh, Jonah walked in the room. Ana would be in tears, he had no doubt. He'd seen the frightened and anxious look on her face. *How do you persuade her that that was just a piece of bad luck? That it wouldn't happen to me. How!*

TEARS RAN FROM ANA'S eyes down her face. Wiping them away with her hand, she tried to smile but her lips trembled. In the time that it had taken Jonah to speak to Mike Benton and turn over the horse and carriage, she had undressed and put on a long sheer camisole. She had been brushing her hair when he walked in. In the corner, a single candle was lit, its tiny flame casting giant shadows on the wall.

There was a tenderness, a feminine softness to her, made more so by the setting. The camisole had a deep neckline that hugged to her full breasts. A faint outline of her nipples was visible at certain angles when she turned. Jonah stood by the small side bar and filled a glass with brandy. He took a swallow just as she moved close to him.

Taking the half full glass, she set it on the table. Her mouth was wide, her lips full, and when she pulled his head down to kiss him, her lips were warmer than the brandy he'd just drunk drunk. The kiss was long and passionate. Her full breasts rose and fell with her breathing. She broke away from the kiss, and still holding his hand, she led him to the bed. As Jonah quickly undressed, she put out the candle. The moon filtered its way past the gnarled limbs of the old oaks surrounding the courtyard, and through the lacy curtains on their bedroom window. It seemed to glow on Ana's hair and her breasts as she removed her camisole.

As the two came together, she whispered, "I want to have your baby."

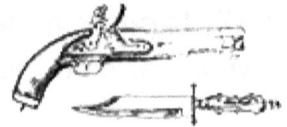

CHAPTER TWENTY ONE

THE TWENTY-SIXTH OF DECEMBER was almost a repeat of the day before. The British were preparing for something, but what? Jackson continued to fortify his defenses. Cotton bales were brought off a ship, creating a scene with the owner. Jackson took a gun from a soldier and thrust it at the man.

"Since they are your property, sir, there's all the more reason for you to defend them," Jackson said. This caused several of the soldiers to snicker, making the man fume all the more. Jackson had sent for Henry Parrish, Rick Smith, Scrap, and the Choctaw leader, Juzan. "I have to know what the British are doing," he explained. "Henry, you take a few Indians and scout the Chef Mentour Road. Richard, you take two of these men and scout the bayous that they take going back to their ships. Juzan, you go with Mr. Smith. Scrap, you take your party and watch the river and the levee."

To send the scouts out in broad daylight was risky, Jonah thought. Jackson knew it, but aside from a few reconnaissances in force and a few cannon balls, one would have thought the British were taking a holiday. So many sentries had been captured that the British no longer posted single sentries. They were now in groups of two or three. Still, Richard Smith and an Indian scout had managed to strike suddenly and swiftly, taking three of them at once. The Indian scout, feeling a bit of devilment in him, took some of the black soggy soil and pushed it down the barrel of two muskets. It was pushed down so far that it sat on top of the ball. He then carefully wiped the evidence away from the bore and left one gun propped against a tree and the other lying on a palmetto bush. A soldier, or maybe two, were going to be in for a big surprise if they didn't check the muskets well before firing them.

The day went on with very little British activity. It was dark when Henry and his two Indians returned. Scrap returned with his two braves an hour later. There was still no sign of Smith and Juzan. It was nearly ten p.m. and Smith still hadn't returned.

Jonah approached Jackson and volunteered, "Moses and I can follow the route Richard and Juzan took, General, while Donnie and Tim can ease along the levee and river."

Jackson was tempted but didn't want to lose any more men, especially the president's man. That night, Jonah and Moses stayed at the camp. There was an air of expectancy about the camp. Jonah looked about at the men. Since working to improve the defenses, most of them looked soiled, dark, and dingy. From the brightly colored pantaloons of LaFitte's men, to the buckskinned volunteers from Tennessee and Kentucky, to the regular army blue and civilian's attire of the New Orleans volunteers, they all looked strained and tired. Enlisted and officers alike, everyone had done his duty. Men sat around little campfires trying to stay warm in the chilly December night.

Stars shined brightly overhead but Donnie swore his knees were telling him it was going to rain…or worse. One of LaFitte's men came by and recognized Jonah and Moses from their visit at Grand Terra with Cooper Cain and Captain Taylor. He passed his bottle of strong rum around for each man to take a drink.

When Jonah went to hand it back, the smuggler gave a wry grin, "Keep it. Dominique will have more."

"Where is Dominique?" Jonah asked.

"He's set up some old sail canvas and has settled down under it beside his baby."

"Baby?" Donnie asked.

"Aye, his big gun what fires huge balls. It is a thirty-two pounder, I believe."

Tim remarked, as the smuggler walked off, "It's strange bedfellows we have."

Using the man's term, Jonah replied, "Aye, but whom better than those to man the cannons. I doubt anyone else has had the experience that they have."

"That's true," Moses added. "I heard the artillery major say that Dominique and Pierre were both masters at their trade."

Tim laughed, "They'd have to be to roll in all the plunder they got. Makes you wonder why they are willing to help after that fool governor and Commodore Patterson pulled what they did."

"I haven't heard a person complain about the cost of their merchandise or slaves," Donnie said. "I can see where the governor felt he had to uphold the law. Sometimes I reckon popular opinions and the law don't always walk the same path."

"That's true," Tim responded. "Right now the path to my blanket is the one I'm taking."

"Let's have one more pull from that bottle first," Moses suggested.

※

Moses and Jonah both rose up with a start. Something was wrong. Jonah could hear excited voices and men moving about quickly. He paused to listen but couldn't make out what any of the voices were saying.

Jonah looked over at Moses and said, "I'm going over to the headquarters' door."

The headquarters was lit up. Entering the building, he was almost run over by one of the general's aides. He walked up to Captain Reid and whispered, "What's all the commotion about?"

"Richard Smith and Juzan have just gotten back. The British are bringing in large guns and they are setting them up on the levee. They plan to fire heated balls at our ships."

"When?" Jonah asked.

"Now, at dawn," Richard replied.

"Damnation," Jonah cursed. "What took so long to get the intelligence to us?"

"They've been stranded up in a tree, watching a steady influx of big guns, powder, and shot, plus a furnace of sorts."

Furnace, Jonah thought. He then realized it was to heat the shot.

"Jackson sent word yesterday for the ship to retire up river but the current was too strong and the wind was too feeble," Richard said.

Suddenly the stillness of the dawn was broken by a thunderous crash. One followed another and flaming red streaks swept through the sky.

"Almost like a comet," Moses muttered.

The guns going off woke up the army. Men were up and moving, lining up behind their barriers. The roar of the guns made it plain that this was ordnance from a larger bore gun than they'd previously faced. Jonah noted that Mike Benton was there with a sketch pad and charcoal in hand. *He must have spent the night at Headquarters*, Jonah thought. He'd not seen the artist since just after dusk yesterday. Jonah felt a pang of guilt until he realized Benton had eaten better and slept with a roof over his head.

"Is this what you were after, Mike?"

Benton smiled, "A tad early for my liking, but where else would I see such a display."

The sounds of the heated shot could be heard striking into the timbers of the gunboat *Carolina*. Men aboard the gunboat tried to fight the flames but with the hull being pierced time and time again, it soon proved to be a fruitless battle. Men were told to abandon ship by the ship's commander, Captain Henley. They had put up a returning fire as best as they could, aiming at flashes from the British gun, but it was now time to get off the roaring furnace that had been a gunboat.

The British cheering suddenly was hushed when one of *Carolina's* last balls found its mark, driving the British gunners behind the protective levee. Both the British and American armies watched in dismay at the unequal battle. Behind the *Carolina*, the *Louisiana* had received an emphatic order to move now. Long boats were in the water with ropes attached to the ship towing it upstream out of range. Still the single gun on the *Carolina* fired on, the gun crew braving the flames, much to the dismay of all who watched. It was a little after sunrise, with the flames towering skyward that the twelve pounder ceased to fire and quickly thereafter a British shot hit the magazine and the ship blew up. A hissing sound was heard over the water as burning debris settled into the muddy Mississippi.

Jonah was standing in the room when Captain Henley reported to Jackson. "The furious cannonade by the British sent hot balls roaring about. They penetrated her hole, my cabin, flaming rigging, and spars were brought down about the crew's ears but they did not want to give up. Half an hour of this work was all it took. A hot ball passed through the filling-room, which contained a considerable amount of powder. All the bulwarks had been shot away and with the vessel sinking I ordered the crew to abandon ship."

"Your losses?" Jackson asked the captain.

"One man killed and six wounded, General," the captain replied.

Jackson nodded and then noted a smile appeared on the captain's face. "Something amuses you, Captain?"

"Ah…no sir. I was just thinking for all the British's efforts, we only lost one twelve pounder gun."

Jackson smiled this time. "Thank you, Captain. You handled yourself most appropriately."

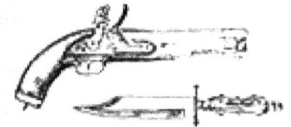

CHAPTER TWENTY TWO

THE EXPLOSION THAT OCCURRED when a hot ball hit *Carolina's* magazine was horrific. Burning fragments filled the air, some raining down on the *Louisiana,* now up river a mile away. While Captain Henley made light that it was only one twelve pounder gun lost, seeing the schooner take such a beating and then blow up had a negative impact on the Americans, while the British cheered. *But they could cheer all they want*, Jonah thought and said as much to Mike Benton, "We'll see who cheers in the end."

The *Louisiana* was still afloat, as were the others, all with much more firepower. The loss of the *Carolina* was demoralizing, but in truth, the British had achieved very little for all their efforts. Jonah wasn't very concerned about the ship's loss. He had been with Commodore Perry on the Great Lakes and knew first hand that one ship does not mean a battle is won. His concern was the explosion. The terrific explosion undoubtedly was heard in New Orleans. What would the town's people think? What would Ana think?

Jonah went to the headquarters to mention to Jackson the need of sending a messenger to New Orleans to tell all was well. Once inside the building, Jonah got in line as several men had been called to carry out Jackson's orders. Officers were sent to fortify certain positions in the line that Jackson was not happy with. Jackson sent off one of the militia men, a local man, to open a section in a drainage canal. He wanted to flood the low-lying field that the British had to cross. It would also flood the ditch that had been dug, making a parapet that his forces used as protection. Doing that would make something of a moat. *It was ingenious how Jackson could think of such things in the planning of his defense*, Jonah thought. A twelve-pound howitzer was ordered to be situated along a section of the line so as to command the high road. A twenty-four pound was placed along the left line to shoulder up the defenses there and when it was discovered there were two of the large howitzers left, they were added to the left line as well.

The crew of the *Carolina* hurried along to assist the Baratarians under Dominique Youx and another of LaFittes men, Renato Beluche. The lines nearest the river were the strongest and best protected. The lines nearest the cypress swamp were the weakest. Men were sent out with picks and shovels to raise the embankment and deepen the canals, making them ready to flood. Coffee's Tennesseans would hold this line. There was no doubt in Jackson's mind that if the defenses were built as they should be, neither hell nor high water would budge Coffee's men.

While Jackson put his men to work, the British commander fortified his position. Ten more guns were brought into the field. Stores and ammunition, powder, and shot were also brought in. General Pakenham's biggest mistake, one he'd realize much too late, was the belief that destroying the *Carolina* removed all significant obstacles from his advance. The advance would start at dawn tomorrow, the twenty-eighth of December, 1814.

The last man in front of Jonah waiting to see Jackson was his friend, Richard Smith. "Mr. Smith," Jackson spoke. "I'd like for you to put together a group of riflemen. Divide them up into three men units and sneak down behind the British lines. Not where you can be boxed in or cut off, but where you can harass the enemy, maybe in relays. I want the British kept awake all night long. If you kill or wound the enemy so much the better, but I want them kept awake, afraid to go to sleep. Move about, find different targets. If they send out troops, retreat until they give up. Remember, whether you hit anybody or not, it's the harassment I'm after."

When Smith departed, Jackson acknowledged Jonah, "I see you've been patiently waiting, Jonah. What can I do for the president's man?"

Smiling, Jonah replied, "Just watching a real general at work, sir."

"Flattery!" Jackson responded. "You must have something in mind."

All the while Jackson had been speaking; one orderly after another had been pushing something in front of him. Mostly, it had been paperwork but now one orderly brought some cut meats and cheese with a slice of bread.

"The last of your ham," Jackson said, indicating the meat that had been cut into chunks. He then paused and looked at Jonah, as if to say 'well.'

Jonah came straight to the point, "The earth shattering explosion of the *Carolina* was bound to have been heard in New Orleans, sir. I wondered if it might not be good to send someone to the city to let everyone know all is well and there's no cause to panic."

Jackson chewed his food in silence and then took a drink of water. "It would need to be an officer," Jackson said, setting the water glass down. "Or...you."

"I was not recommending that I be the messenger, General."

"I didn't think you were, but whom better than you," Jackson responded. "I don't think it's any longer a secret that you are Madison's man. I don't mean that in any negative manner, Jonah. In truth, I've come to appreciate you and enjoy our times together. No, I can't think of a better person, and you are right, of course. Unless the governor hears all is well, he'll be here himself. Go, Jonah, bear the good news and take one of your scalawags with you so they can be putting the word out to the common man, while you wait upon the governor."

"Yes, sir," Jonah responded.

"Jonah."

"Sir."

"Kiss Ana, and give her my regards, and one last thing, Jonah. Be back before first light. I feel tomorrow Pakenham will attack. I will have sentries along the main road. Make sure you don't surprise anyone and get shot."

"Yes, sir!"

JONAH AND MOSES HAD only gotten a mile down the road when they met the first of the city's prominent citizens coming out to check on the explosion. Riding together were the lawyers, Livingston and Meeks, and behind them in a carriage was Captain Eli Taylor's banker, but Jonah couldn't remember his name. Jonah gave the men a quick narrative of the events that had led up to the destruction of the *Carolina*.

"Why did they go after a gunboat, instead of the ship?" Meeks asked.

Before Jonah could answer, Livingston quickly said, "We need to be thankful that they didn't."

"That's true," Meeks and the banker replied.

As everyone turned to head back to New Orleans, the banker spoke to Jonah. "Captain Taylor tells me your father has joined in on a couple of shipping ventures."

Not sure of how much business it was of the banker's, obviously it was some, or Taylor wouldn't have told him. Jonah just replied, "Yes sir."

"The privateer, young Cooper Cain's, command has proven to be a good investment. I was not sure someone so young should be the captain, but he has proven his worth."

So Cooper is nothing more than an investment to this man. The thought angered Jonah, but he kept silent. Taylor had included the banker in the *SeaFire* venture. This made Jonah pause to wonder if the banker had been an investor in any of the captain's pirate endeavors. It was none of his business so he didn't ask.

Several other groups were met on the way to town. One of which was determined to make an inspection of Jackson's defenses. When it appeared he couldn't dissuade the old French general from going, Jonah took another route.

"Make sure to stop your carriage about a mile from camp and have your man wait while you walk in. Jackson is in need of horses and wagons. Also carry your weapons, as the British are expected to attack at any minute and you may find yourself conscripted and standing the line.

After a second or two of clearing his throat, the old Frenchman said, "I hear M'sieur General Jackson is a competent authority. I will leave it up to him."

Meeks and Livingston smiled, "You are a silver tongue rogue, Mr. Lee. No wonder Jackson likes you, even if you are Madison's man."

"Agent," Jonah corrected. "I'm my own man."

Both nodded with Meeks saying, "No offense meant, sir."

"None taken," Jonah replied.

The narrative of *Carolina's* destruction was repeated several more times as people met them. The people then turned and headed back to the city.

Mr. Livingston volunteered to accompany Jonah to Claiborne's house. Taking the lawyer up on his offer, Jonah asked Moses to go tell Ana that all was well and he'd be there directly. When the two men were alone, Mr. Livingston inquired about the Baratarians. When Jonah spoke well of them, he pulled his horse up, Jonah reining in as well.

"Sir," Livingston began. "It would do my heart good if you could find a way to speak positively about those good men."

Smiling, Jonah caught the lawyer's drift. A poke in the governor's eye, it would be. "Rest assured, Mr. Livingston, I will do my utmost to drive their dedication to duty and country home. I may even mention

I'm going to recommend to the president that they receive the recognition due them."

Livingston was smiling now, "I knew you and I were cut from the same mold, Jonah. Be assured I will always be at your service, sir."

PART IV

Yeah, they ran through the briers and they ran through the brambles
They ran through the bushes where a rabbit couldn't go
They ran so fast that the hounds couldn't catch 'em
On down the Mississippi to the Gulf of Mexico

We fired our cannon till the barrel melted down
So we grabbed an alligator and we fought another round
We filled his head with cannon balls 'n' powdered his behind
And when we touched the powder off, the gator lost his mind.

PART IV

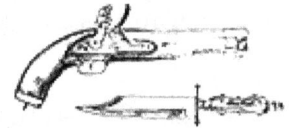

CHAPTER TWENTY THREE

THE MORNING HAD A chill to it as Jonah sat in the kitchen eating a leftover pastry and drinking black chicory coffee in the hopes that it would wake him up. The cook was preparing things to fix for breakfast for the hotel guests. Ana, in a long housecoat, sat next to him. When Moses came in, the cold wind caused her to shiver and pull the neck of her housecoat closer.

Shutting the door quickly, Moses said, "Sorry." He sat down and dug into a sticky pastry, dunking it in the steaming coffee.

"You shor you don't want nuthin' to eat, honey?" the morning cook asked. "These heah men ain't got no manners, way they dig in and don't ask what you'd like."

Moses suddenly felt guilty, but Jonah just smiled. "It ain't nine o'clock, Miss Suzy. She rarely eats before then."

"Huh," Suzy snorted. "Mannered man would ask anyway."

Jonah stood up and took Ana's hand, then very politely asked, "Sweetheart is there anything you'd like? Coffee, cocoa, a pastry... anything."

It was Ana who was smiling now at her man's outrageous display. "No, silly!"

Jonah bowed, kissed her hand and sat down. "See, Miss Suzy, she doesn't want anything."

"Hush, you...you ole stinker. I got work to do. I ain't got no time for yo' foolishness." She then turned to Moses, "And yor's either."

Moses swallowed hard and looked up. "What'd I do?"

When the hasty breakfast was over, Moses volunteered, "You're going to need a heavy coat today. May even sleet some, air has a devilish feel to it."

Jonah's heaviest coat was not a real cold weather coat. Something he'd have to get if one was available in New Orleans. As Moses brought the horses around, Jonah said goodbye to Ana.

She was not as fearful now as she seemed last evening. She had been beside herself with fear when Moses returned. Her first words had been, "Where's Jonah?"

"He's fine," Moses quickly informed her. "He had to run by the governor's house first on an errand for the general."

When Jonah had made it home, he'd eaten, got a bath and when they went to bed, she had whispered, "Hold me, Jonah." They had fallen asleep with her curled up against him. *I hope this war ends soon,* Jonah thought.

JONAH REPORTED TO GENERAL Jackson as soon as they got to headquarters. After that, he and Moses spotted a fire that several of their friends had surrounded, trying to keep warm. Scrap, Richard Smith, Henry Parrish, and the Hall's stood in a circle, hands thrust out toward the flames.

"Umm...somebody smells good," Scrap volunteered.

Smith bent forward and sniffed a time or two. "You ain't turning funny on us, are you, Jonah?"

"No, I'm not. While you were bedded up with the gators and such, I was sleeping on clean sheets with a beautiful woman."

"Whew," Donnie said, in an exaggerated way. "I'm shore glad to hear that. I was worried there for a minute."

Jonah gave his friend a good-natured shove and then asked, "How did your night go?"

Now everyone was in smiles. "We pestered them a mite," Scrap swore.

"More'n a mite," Tim said. "They got so they'd jump and call sergeant of the guard at every sound."

"Andy said that he wanted them Redcoats 'hare rassed,'" Scrap started. "I'd say we made some of them pur-tee miserable. We started off with Juzan shooting a couple burning arrows into some tents. Quick as he let go with his arrow, he skedaddled. One of the other Injuns kilt a sentry and scalped him. Smith took a couple of shots at their cannon, pinging balls off and them ricocheting. I shimmied up a tree and every time two sentries walked past one another, I'd chunk a pine cone, hitting first one and then the other. Later at another tree, me and one of them Injuns tossed a rope down on a sodger and then jumped down holding on to the rope and pulling him up into the tree. We tied it off and then hid. He was just spittin' and sputtering when his sergeant got there. When the sergeant went to untie that sodger, my Choctaw threw his tomahawk chopping off a finger and cutting the rope in two, causing the hanging sodjer to fall on his sergeant, who was nursing his hand. An ossifer come running up with a squad of men then. Some got down into the swamp and stuck in the muck having to have help to get out. As the men spread out, I laid my barrel along someone's noggin."

"We shot into a couple of campfires that was closer to the trees, sending debris about," Smith added. "All told probably killed two or three, wounded maybe six and aggravated most of a regiment.

"He ain't telling it all," Scrap said. "This major was holding a tin cup of coffee in his hand, while talking to a captain. When the major tilted the cup of coffee up to take a drink, Smith shot the cup out of his hand, spilling coffee all over that clean sodger suit." Everyone was laughing now. "Not to mention, ruining a perfectly good cup," Scrap added. This even had Smith laughing.

Jackson, who was standing at a window, heard the men laughing. "Hear that," he said, addressing General Coffee and Captain Lieupo.

"When our men are able to find something to laugh at on a cold December morning like this, there's no way we can lose."

Captain Lieupo smiled, "I know the sound of a few of them, General. Jonah and Moses are in that bunch."

"He's a well liked man," Jackson said, and then added, "both he and Moses."

"He's a good soldier as well, General, but of course, you know that," Lieupo said.

"Yes, I do, Captain. Were he in uniform, he'd probably be the one in command."

"I don't think so, General. I think Jonah would be the first to say the right man is in charge."

Jackson was silent a moment, and then added, "I think you are right, but he's not afraid to speak his mind or tell me when he thinks I'm wrong."

"Well, General, part of that's doing what he was assigned to do by President Madison. But for the most part, that's Jonah. You don't ask what he thinks unless you really want to hear it. And…if he feels strong enough about something, you're likely to hear about it without asking. That's probably why he ain't in uniform. He told General Harrison off a time or two when they were up in the northwest. Colonel Richard M. Johnson said that he had never seen anyone stand up to a general like Jonah did. Johnson also said that Jonah told General Harrison the British were now on the run, it was time to get off his arse and give chase before they could reorganize. It's said he went with Commodore Perry to battle the British on the Great Lakes. Yes, sir, but Moses said when he got back on land he admitted he had little desire for that sort of fighting again."

Jackson smiling, responded, "Nor I."

Captain Lieupo looked around and made sure no one was listening. "I have it from Major Hampton's mouth, General, that it was Jonah who killed Tecumseh, not Colonel Richard Mentor Johnson, who's been given the credit. The major said Johnson was so badly wounded, he couldn't hold up his rifle to take aim. Tecumseh was drawing down on the colonel when Jonah shot him. Only the colonel's rifle went off almost at the same time but the ball went into the ground. Some soldier saw Johnson fire, saw Tecumseh fall and started shouting that the colonel had killed him."

"I don't think I've ever heard him say he killed Tecumseh," Jackson said.

"No, sir, me neither, but you ain't heard him say he didn't either."

"No, you're right there, Captain."

At that time, other men entered the room and Jackson turned his attention to them, but he was also thinking, *that's another aspect of Jonah that I hadn't known. Should I ever seek the presidency, that's a man I'd like to have on hand, one who wasn't prone to brag.* It was known that Johnson had a spy network and contacts everywhere. No wonder he'd been more than willing to put out the word about Ana. Not many men would go to that extreme or expense, just for the hell of it. No, Jonah did the proud colonel a good service by letting him take the credit for killing the war chief, Tecumseh. This could very well help the man in politics. By his not verbally claiming the kill he would seem to be shying away from the glory and thereby making him a stronger candidate. Something to keep in mind, Jackson thought. Something to keep in mind.

THE MORNING OF DECEMBER 28th was like many winter days in the Deep South. Heavy dew had fallen the night before. It hung on the leaves and moss in the oak and cypress trees. As the sun came up, the forest literally sparkled like a diamond held to a light. Drops of the dew fell off the needles of the evergreen trees. Some dropping on hats, shirts, and even going down the neck of a few, causing a quick shiver.

Smith had reported the constant coming and goings of boats, bringing in more supplies...food, powder, and shot. A couple more pieces of artillery had been brought in as well.

"They'll fight today," Jonah volunteered to the men standing around the fire.

"It's time we get 'em," Donnie complained. "I don't mind a good ruckus but it's turning near winter and we's thangs to get done at home. I told Peggy we'd help whoop the Redcoats and get on back. I didn't know they'd be so durned slow about fighting."

Tim smiled at his daddy. "He's probably got a hankering for some of ma's cooking."

"The Redcoats are moving," someone shouted.

Looking out across the field, skirmishes were seen. Bending low to make themselves smaller targets, they moved across the plain. Using his small telescope, Jonah scanned the horizon. Men were mounting their horses and others were gathering around the artillery. Overhead the sun climbed and its brightness caused vapors in patches as the dew dried.

"Reckon we'll get tested today," Moses said, laying a hand on Jonah's shoulder.

Jonah put his hand on Moses' arm, "Keep your head down, brother."

Moses smiled, "You as well. I don't want you to mess up that pretty face before you marry Ana. Could be after all this trouble to find her, she might choose someone with a prettier face."

Jonah gently punched Moses on the arm. "Well, it won't be you." They both chuckled.

At that time, Mike Benton walked up. He had a pad of paper in his hand and his pockets were full of charcoal pens and chalk. "Captain Reid said I should attach myself to you," Benton volunteered. "He said the two of you usually wind up in the thick of it."

"If that be true, let's me and you find a safer place," Donnie said to Tim.

"Humph! A while ago you were chomping at the bit to get this done, now you're looking for safer ground," Tim responded. He then turned to his friends, "Don't mind pa. You couldn't drag him away with a brace of mules."

Birds were starting to move about and calling to each other. "Mockingbird," Scrap said.

On the British lines, General Pakenham called his officers together. "A grand reconnaissance will be the order for today. With any luck, we'll be able to leap over these backward people and ride on in to New Orleans." *And the House of Lords for me*, he thought, but did not say.

Jackson would not be caught unaware. He'd had his scouts out and listened to their reports. Yet he'd taken his telescope to the upper floor of his headquarters. He had five cannons ready to use where the biggest mass of British seemed to be gathering. Dominque Youx, Beluche, and several Baratarians were in charge of two of his big guns, while the others were manned by the crew from the sunken *Carolina*. One was under the command of Lieutenant Crawley and Lieutenant Norris, while the artillery captain, Captain Humphrey, and his artillerymen had the other. They were ready and capable, this Jackson knew. They'd stand until every gun was empty or they were dead. Upstream, the *Louisiana* swung on her cable, ready to add her weight to the battle when the time came.

The British had just passed the Chalmette and Bienvenue homes. Only five hundred yards to go and he'd give the order. Turning to Captain Reid, Jackson said, "Get my horse. We'll go down."

General John Coffee saluted Jackson as he came down the stairs. "I'm about to join my men, Andy." Jackson smiled. He and Coffee were best of friends. They had been several campaigns together. It was only at times like this that he spoke informally.

"Have a care," Jackson replied, and the two shook hands briefly.

Captain Reid watched but didn't say a word. Jackson was a natural leader, but General Coffee was no slouch either.

THE BRITISH ADVANCE WAS breathtaking, a spectacle in the extreme. Mike Benton's fingers fairly flew as he attempted to catch as much of the splendid advance as possible before the battle truly started. Men gathered behind their defenses. Mud walls stood shoulder high with cotton bales and wood intermixed. Below the mud walls was a flooded ditch several feet wide, and before the ditch there was a field of mud. To get to the top of the mud walls, soldiers would have to use ladders or climb over one another while the Americans poured down a deadly fire. Not being a military man, it was still easy for Benton to see it would be suicide to try to take this position. Were he the British general, he'd find another place to land and strike quickly before Jackson had a chance to dig in.

Forward they came, with the sun shining down on their bright red uniforms. In tight formation, in such an orderly manner, the British marched. A screeching sound was heard overhead as rockets filled the air.

"Children's toys," Jackson shouted as several nervous men began to back away from their positions. Jackson rode up on his horse and repeated his words, "Children's toys made to frighten you." As he sat up on his horse unmoved by the shower of rockets, men fell back in place.

The roar of cannons was now being heard. The guns were located at the British forward positions and on the levee. For Mike Benton and several of the citizen soldiers from New Orleans, the sight was certainly imposing. It was a formidable display of military might and discipline. The mighty British army was now ready to fight.

The sun glinted on the British muskets so that at times it was almost blinding to watch. Jackson had ordered Hinds to withdraw before they could be fired upon. His dragoons had been sent out to observe. Seeing this force flee without a shot being fired at them gave the British heart.

Standing behind the line, Jonah explained to Benton, "Jackson doesn't want them in the way when we start to fire. We don't need anybody killed by friendly fire."

"Understand," Benton replied. For the first time then, it came to him. It may look like a show right now, but soon the show would be over and men would die. On both sides, men would die.

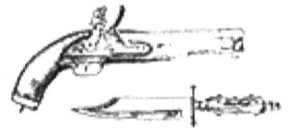

CHAPTER TWENTY FOUR

As the British continued to advance, the Americans stood behind their breastworks. Near the river, a few houses blocked the view of the oncoming British from the American defense, just as they had blocked the Americans from seeing the Redcoats. Passing the houses, the British could now see the cannons lined up on the road and the partial view of the American gunboats. Once the end of the British troops passed the houses, the Americans would open up.

Jonah had just whispered to Benton, "Any time now." Why the whisper Benton wondered, and then realized all the laughter, bawdy jokes, and jeering had ceased.

Richard Smith, who had been away on an errand, slid into position with his friends. "Captain Lieupo sends his best," Smith said.

"Where is he?" Scrap asked.

"Acting as messenger for the general," Smith replied.

Hampered by a severe limp, Lieupo could still ride a horse. Jackson was employing the man where he was best suited, a larger target sitting on a horse, still a needed…a necessary job. One Captain Steve Lieupo would carry out to his utmost ability.

Jonah said a small prayer for his friends' safety. Only the prayer was cut short…interrupted by the sound of the American fire. His mind being on his prayer, he'd not heard the order to fire.

The gunners had been ready…anticipating the order, the roar of the cannons with flames belching forth were let loose, echoing the general's order to fire. Not to be outdone by the shore artillery, the ships opened up. The bang of the muskets was drowned out by the roar of the bigger guns. Yet the withering fire from the American marksmen had its effect.

"Scrap…you ain't even aiming," Donnie accused.

"Don't need to," Scrap replied, while ramming a ball down the barrel of his long rifle. "There's so many, I just shoot amongst them and it'll hit somebody." This caused the group to smile.

While the Americans were laying down a withering fire, very few of the British balls were striking home, due to their high mud breastworks.

"Bet them that complained about Jackson's insistence on the high, thick defenses are thanking him now," Moses shouted to Jonah. Due to the noise, Jonah didn't reply but nodded as he reloaded his rifle.

Dominique Youx and his crew manned the cannons nearest to where Jonah's group fought. Jonah glanced their way and then looked back. All the guns' crew had bandanas tied around their head covering their ears. That was a giveaway of their ship training. He'd noticed Commodore Perry's gunners doing the same. He couldn't see the army artillerymen but wondered if they were doing the same thing.

The horror of the battlefield showed itself to Mike Benton. It was a scarce cannonball that fell short of its target. Between the sounds of the cannons, the loud click of hammers on long rifles could be heard preceding the bang of the guns. Some of the American guns had been loaded with hot balls and fired at outbuildings the Redcoats were using for cover. The British were caught between the raging flames of the fires and the onslaught of American cannons and rifle fire. Shrieks and the cries of the wounded could be heard over the din of battle. The sound was almost sickening to the artist. Still it was a full half an hour before the attack was called off and then only after two field pieces and one mortar were hit by the deadly American forces. The guns were dismounted and entire crews were killed, some by their own exploding ordinance.

Before the British artillery was silenced, the Redcoats had marched all the way to the canal where they were halted and had to give up the day. The British did not turn in regimental formation as they had so boldly marched forward. As there had been no flag of surrender, the men ran as individuals back to their camp. The ground battle had not lasted an hour, but it was late afternoon before the retreating Redcoats had all made it to the relative safety of their camp with their wounded.

When Commodore Patterson reported to Jackson that evening, it was as though he had singly repulsed the British attack. He related they'd been fired upon until four p.m. but without anything other than shell fragments touching the ship. He also related that in the seven hours of the enemy attack he'd fired eight hundred rounds from the *Louisiana's* guns with only one man wounded.

Jackson was to learn later in the evening that Pakenham's reconnaissance in force, as he now called it, cost him nearly sixty men killed.

As the Americans retreated to their campfires, their spirits were high. A few bottles and jugs were broached and while no man drank enough to get drunk, it helped ease the battle lust that filled the men. The men started back with their bawdy stories and jokes. They'd had a taste of battle and they now were thankful to be alive.

As Benton looked at the men around his fire he was amazed. A white man, educated and the president's agent, a black and Indian mix who the president's man called brother, and who seemed to be much more educated than most of the others. A refined Richard Smith, who scouted for Jackson, and three men who obviously felt more at home in the backwoods but didn't seem out of place in the dining room at Hotel Provincial. These were the men who camped together, fought together, and yes some who would die together. This was what made the American Forces, and he was a part of it. Taking out his drawing pad and sitting by the fire, he drew the men. Their faces powder blackened and streaked with sweat. *What a picture*, he thought.

CHAPTER TWENTY FIVE

THE DAY'S RESOUNDING VICTORY, though, was dimmed that evening when General Carroll reported. A British detachment under Colonel Rennie had advanced upon Jackson's extreme left line. The embankment was the least in all of Jackson's defenses and was a place where the ditch could be leapt. When British General Gibbs sighted the area, he did not order a full-scale attack, as this was strictly a reconnaissance. He did allow Colonel Rennie to advance upon the rude line of defense.

Seeing the British advance, General Carroll allowed Colonel Henderson to lead a column of two hundred Tennesseans along the border of the swamp in an attempt to cut off the Redcoats. However, the British had left troops concealed in the woods to protect their retreat. Seeing Henderson's men, they cut loose. Now, it was Henderson who was hemmed in. The British opened fire, and Colonel Henderson and five of his troops were killed with the first volley. The Americans made a hasty retreat and in the confusion Colonel Rennie could have taken the line had not General Gibbs ordered him to retire from the field.

To say Jackson was furious was an understatement. With his fury finally exhausted, he faced General Carroll and calmly said, "You are lucky, Divine Providence smiled down on us today."

Matters were made worse when Colonel Declouet rushed into the camp with news that rumor was the State Legislature was mediating a scheme to surrender the city to the British. Jackson was out riding to General Coffee's area of defense when the news came in. Colonel

Declouet therefore relayed the information to one of Jackson's aides, Mr. Abner L. Duncan.

Mr. Duncan rushed to inform Jackson. Seeing Duncan approach in such an agitated state, Jackson reined in his horse. For the second time that day, Jonah watched as Jackson became livid.

"Have you seen the letter?" Jackson demanded.

"No sir."

"Who gave you this information?" Jackson barked.

"Colonel Declouet, General."

"Where is Colonel Declouet?" Before Duncan could reply, Jackson snarled, "If this intelligence is true, the good colonel ought to be arrested and shot." Again Jackson asked, "Where is Declouet?"

"He went back to New Orleans," Duncan replied.

"I don't believe this," Jackson hissed.

"What should I tell the governor?" Duncan asked meekly.

As the general had turned his horse, he stopped, turned and rested his hand on the horse's back, "Tell the governor to make a strict inquiry into the subject, and if they persist...blow them up."

All along the line, men began to cheer and take up the chant...Blow them up! Blow them up! Blow them up!

THE NEXT FEW DAYS were almost boring. The British showed no inclination to face a similar fate as their first reconnaissance in force. Neither did they test the extreme left line, where Jackson had increased the number of defenders.

Jonah spent several days in New Orleans. At night, he joined his friends and formed 'hunting parties', along with the Choctaws. Every night the parties went out killing and wounding the sentinels. Scrap killed three in one night, and brought back the soldiers' weapons and items of interest. Most of the items were sold or traded to the Choctaws. The morale of the Redcoats was turning sour. To stand alone on the picket line meant sure death.

One of the Choctaws was a half-breed named Poindexter. His father had been a trader and his mother was the chief's daughter. Poindexter sat with a group of scouts one night. He'd killed five Redcoats in three nights, and like Scrap he had the plunder to show for his efforts, but was unhappy about not being able to take scalps.

"Why?" Scrap questioned.

"Captain Jugeat has forbidden scalping," Poindexter replied. "Officer gives me this, not a scalp, but it will help to pass the cold nights with good friends." With that being said, he brought out a full flask and passed it around. When the whiskey was finished, Poindexter stood up and started to leave.

"Where you going?" Moses asked.

"Get more trade items," he said. "Officers like Redcoats' guns, me like money and whiskey. Soon I be rich, you wait and see."

Richard Smith laughed, "In an Indian fashion, he will be a big man soon if he doesn't get shot."

"He'd be a bigger man, if he could take a few scalps," Scrap threw out. "Might be I'll get a few and give them to him. Andy ain't done told us *us* not too." Everyone laughed but Jonah wasn't too sure Scrap didn't mean it.

It was New Year's Day, January 1st, 1815. Jackson had been up early and broken his fast. Scouts had reported hammering going on in the British camp, but on what was the question. Jonah, Moses, Richard Smith, and the Halls were trying to stay warm next to a fire. The fog was and had been so dense that the Redcoats' camp was not visible at all.

Jackson's aide, Captain Reid, had ridden up with a written invitation for Jonah to join the general for a noontime meal, should the state of affairs allow it…meaning if they were not in battle. Donnie and Scrap were betting how long it would be before the British advanced.

Scrap bet it would be at sunup, while Donnie felt it'd be after the fog had lifted.

"Either way, we'll smell gunpowder today," Smith said. Moses grunted his agreement.

The hammering had ceased in the enemy camp and it was now quiet.

"Too quiet," Tim said. "Redcoats could be at our line and we wouldn't know it."

"They'll be coming soon," Moses prophesied. "It's always quiet before the thunder. It'll be soon, but I agree with Donnie, the fog has them stalled."

The silence remained unbroken at sunup, eight ò clock, and at nine. The fog still blocked all visibility of the British camp. Men that had sat tightly, grim and prepared at their station, now started to relax.

A young soldier near Dominique Youx's battery pulled his gun off the cotton bale he'd been standing behind and sighed, "Awe hell. This is going to be another day of waiting…waiting for nothin'."

The soldier's attitude was infectious. Some of the officers felt the need to take a break from the toil the men had been put through preparing for the British. After all, it was New Year's Day, Jackson conceded. The men would have a grand review on the open ground between his headquarters and their defensive line.

COMMODORE PATTERSON HAD KEPT the *Louisiana* tied up beyond the enemy's range of fire. He had sent a party of his men to the shore battery that had been established with some of the ship's guns. Right away, the men caught a deserter from the British camp. He informed Patterson of two new huge howitzers that had been established in a battery on the levee. They had also constructed a furnace where the balls could be kept red hot. Patterson knew that should one of the balls hit his ship, it was likely all would be lost.

The commodore, taking advantage of this information, landed two more of the ship's guns with enough men to handle them. All of this was done under the cover of the fog. The deserter was sent to Jackson's headquarters for further questioning.

At the American lines, Jonah and Moses reclined against one of Dominique Youx's cannons, watching the artist, Mike Benton, sketch a scene of the American army. Bands were playing, flags were flying, and officers rode their horses back and forth through the ranks. Jackson and his entourage had yet to make an appearance, but would very soon.

Moses touched Jonah on the arm to get his attention. "Had we known this was to be a day of celebration, we could have stayed in town…and had our own private celebration." Moses had been spending more time with Fawn…or was it the other way around? Sally had been in and out. She'd likely be around when needed but if not, Ana was still well taken care of.

Jonah's train of thought was broken when Dominique spoke, "Damnation, the fog is lifting."

Jonah had just looked at his watch but hadn't realized it was brighter. It was about a quarter to ten. The air was suddenly filled with the thunder of the Redcoats' cannons.

"That was as least a full battery," Dominique swore.

"I counted thirty of their guns," Dominique's gun captain swore.

The blood chilling scream of Congreve rockets filled the air. Even with the sun out, their red flare was visible as they streaked across the sky. The American army, taken completely by surprise, scrambled to the line and their positions.

"They must have found out where Jackson was headquartered," Donnie Hall exclaimed as he and Tim ran up.

"They're shelling the headquarters sure enough," Tim added.

For all the thunder and screams of the Redcoats' cannons and rockets, very few fell on the American lines. Most of the rockets did seem to concentrate on the headquarters' building. Smith and Benton ran up.

"The outbuildings are catching hell," Smith said, "but Jackson's building has received very little damage."

"They'll find it," Moses said.

They did…in ten minutes of bombardment, the plantation house was hit by one hundred balls. Jackson had run out of the building, dusty from the debris. Colonel Butler got knocked down, but was quickly back up on his feet. Both men made it to the lines.

"Never know'd somebody ta get so peeved up over a little band playing," Scrap swore. "Just when I wuz getting in a mind to dance."

Jackson's first stop was at Captain Humphrey's battery, the closest to Dominique Youx. "Ah, all is right," Jackson said. He then added, "Humphrey is at his post and will return their compliments presently." Walking down the line, Jackson paused as Colonel Butler ran up. Jackson had last seen him knocked to the ground. "Why Colonel Butler, is that you," roared the general. "I thought you were killed."

This caused the men to whoop and cheer. Jackson spoke to the men at Youx's battery and then walked up to Jonah. "It appears the British have interrupted our noon meal plans, Jonah."

Jonah said, smiling, "There will be other days, General."

As the fog lifted even more, Captain Humphrey's battery opened up. "Let her off," he ordered. In rapid succession, fifty American guns followed, spitting forth ball and grape.

"It's one hell of a fireworks display for New Year's," Richard Smith threw out.

CHAPTER TWENTY SIX

THE THUNDER FROM THE previous firing of the British cannons was nothing compared to the hell on earth from both camps firing. When Humphrey's cannons fired, so did every gun along the American lines. Jonah felt like a stranger, a man without purpose as he watched Youx's men. Second only to Humphrey, their guns spewed forth their own flaming load of grape on ball...once, twice, even three times a minute, the big guns roared. Jonah, Moses and the two Hall men finally found themselves carrying powder and shot, which seemed to disappear as soon as it was delivered.

Youx's men worked fervently, no one needed instruction. Like gears in a cog, the gunners put forth a display that could have only come from years of experience...of pirating. Naked from the waist up, bandanas around their ears, they fired the cannons. Some even tied rags around their nose and mouth. The stench of acrid smoke filled the air, the nose, and the lungs. The men still didn't slow down.

"How do they keep at it?" Donnie threw out, but nobody replied.

After thirty minutes, Mike Benton laid down his sketch pad and helped carry powder and shot.

Guns along both lines fired ball after ball; howitzers on the levee and Commodore Patterson's batteries, all kept up a continuous firing. The large caliber gun creating such a boom it was surely heard in New Orleans and beyond. For an hour and a half, the barrage continued without pause. Six or eight big guns often fired as one, and there was the continuous crash of balls. *No doubt the civilians were filled with fear*, Jonah thought. But that couldn't be helped. Would some of them gather enough nerve to ride to see the mighty guns duel.

"Some will think its dooms day," Tim Hall shouted as he passed by.

Hopefully, Ana would not venture out, Jonah prayed.

Then, just as it started, it ceased. The men had long since been unable to see the enemy, and had taken to firing at the flashes as flames leapt from the mouths of the cannons. The smoke was so dense, the flash was hardly visible. Yet for all the balls fired, the Americans received very little damage. Most of the Redcoats' balls buried themselves in the soft earth of the embankments that Jackson had pushed the men to build. If anything, it strengthened them. Some of the balls overshot their target and killed men bringing up the powder and shot. One man was returning with powder when a ball struck the powder bag. In a flash, he was incinerated, leaving no evidence that he was even there. Moses tugged on Jonah's shirt as he paused in awe.

After a few minutes of the guns going silent, Captain Steve Lieupo came up and spoke, "We lost a boat full of stores that will be hard to replace."

The merchants in New Orleans were already fussing about all of Jackson's requisitions. Some of the cotton bales had not fared very well from the barrage. Many of them were knocked about, some had even caught on fire, and down the line Jonah could see a man tearing one apart. Once he got the cotton bale torn to his satisfaction, he used it for a cot and laid down on it.

Behind the British lines a powder cart had been hit and blew up, with flames leaping skyward. "Good shot," Dominique had shouted and the men gave a cheer. *Was it really their ball that hit it*, Jonah wondered. There was no way to tell and he would not dispute the Baratarian's claim.

Catching his breath, Mike Benton spoke, "I wondered if the firing would ever stop."

"Had to," Dominique responded. "The guns were too hot to fire. They'd have blown up on us if we had continued much longer." Tubs that had been filled with water to sponge out the guns were now completely dry.

As the tired gunners pulled the rags from their heads, they looked for a place to relax. Some of them just collapsed on the ground beside their gun, others sat on cotton bales, and some of the others leaned against the embankment. A group of the slave women and some volunteers brought around water buckets. A few of the volunteers had cups but most of them had gourd dippers. While the men drank and quenched their parched throats, water ran down their faces causing the black powder soot to streak.

"They look like clowns," Moses whispered to Jonah.

Even though the thunder of guns had ceased, Jonah's ears still roared, "Huh."

"I said that they look like clowns with their faces streaked." This time several men heard. At first they appeared angry, then one person's chuckle had them all laughing.

During the firing, Dominique had been using his glass to direct his gunner's aim. Somehow a fragment from an enemy ball wounded him. While Richard Smith was tying a bandana around the wound, Dominique swore, "I'll make them pay for that." When the bandana was tied, he called out, "Can you see that cannon, Jonah? Keep your eye on it."

Damn, I see a whole line of cannons, Jonah thought. He grunted and watched the line as if he knew exactly which one Dominique meant.

After calling instructions to his men, Dominique gave the order to fire. A big twenty-four pounder in the British line suddenly leaped in the air and killed its entire seven man crew. Dominique turned to Jonah and winked. The man knew his business. It seemed with all of the British guns roaring and balls raining down, there had been but one death to the American army. Jonah wondered if that counted the powder carrier, whose body incinerated, but he didn't ask.

A civilian had been in the wrong place at the wrong time...a Mr. Larborde. Captain Lieupo said, telling the story. "It seems Mr. Larborde was standing behind Phillippe Peddesclaux. When Phillippe couldn't light his cigar, he bent over to try again. As he bent forward, a British ball struck Larborde. I declare, Phillippe swore when he rose up and saw Larborde's prostrate body and realized the man's brains had been splattered across his suit."

Scrap said, "That cigar saved him, lucky idjit."

Lieupo also told how a Major Carmick, who commanded the volunteer battalion, was riding over to speak to Jackson. The general had been on his horse riding up and down the line during the entire artillery barrage. As the major neared the general, he was knocked off his horse by a Congreve rocket, which struck him on the forehead. He injured both of his arms, falling off the horse, but received no real injury to his head. One of the men in his battalion shouted, 'His wife said he was a hard-headed soul. Now we know it's true.'

Lieupo spoke just above a whisper then, speaking just to his close friends, "Batteries number one and two were kept in need of powder and ball. As you know, Governor Claiborne was in charge of munitions. When the gun commander ceased firing due to lack of powder and shot, Jackson got so livid that he shouted at Claiborne. 'By the Almighty God, if you do not send me balls and powder instantly, I'll chop off your head and have it rammed into one of those field pieces.'"

Benton, who had heard the comments, asked, "Did they get what they needed?"

Lieupo replied, "Has a cat got a climbing gear?" Now everyone in the group started laughing.

When he could control his laughter, Richard Smith said, "Well, Claiborne still has his head."

"I better be going," Lieupo said, as he got back in his saddle.

"Damned, if he wasn't entertaining," Jonah swore.

"Yeah, it was funny, but I don't 'spect the governor will feel too kindly toward Jackson," Moses volunteered.

"No, he won't, but it'll take men like Jackson to get this war won," Jonah said. "The time for niceties will be after."

"You're right," Moses said, "but grudges start now."

The smoke had almost completely cleared and the British line was again visible.

"Damnation," Dominique Youx swore.

The formidable British batteries, which so defiantly roared out their challenge over an hour and a half ago, were now totally destroyed. The sailors and gunners who had manned them were either dead or had gone behind the lines.

"'Pears we did our work satisfactorily and completely," Beluche shouted over the cheers of the men along the lines, as they could now see the destruction caused by the American guns.

"I know Beluche and Dominique are not the only gun captains out here," Jonah said, speaking to Smith and Moses. "But I'd lay a bet, they out fired and scored more hits than all of the other four batteries put together."

"I'd not take that bet," Smith returned. "Those are men who know their business."

A shadow came up over them. Looking up, Jonah saw Jackson on his horse. *Had he heard our conversation?* Jonah wondered, but only for a moment.

"Taking heed to your council has paid off again, hasn't it, Jonah?" Jackson asked.

Yes, Jackson had heard and was speaking of Jonah's strong recommendation to accept LaFitte and his men's help.

"When you next write our good friend in Washington," Jackson said, meaning the president, "you may wish to compliment our brave volunteers' actions to him."

"I will, General," Jonah replied.

"I will as well," Jackson said as he rode off.

Will he? Jonah wondered. *No doubt he means to, but will he?*

It was like Moses could read Jonah's thoughts. "He will, Jonah, he will."

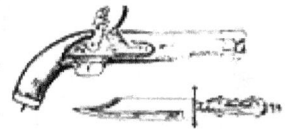

CHAPTER TWENTY SEVEN

When it was apparent that the day's actions were concluded, Jackson sent out a few of his most trusted scouts. This included Richard Smith, Scrap, the Halls and Henry Parrish. Several of the Indians were sent out as well. However, Jackson desired concise and accurate reports that could only be furnished by his backwoodsmen.

A late afternoon meal was scheduled with Jonah being already invited. *Damnation,* Jonah thought, *I'd much rather ride back to New Orleans.*

"I'll go," Moses volunteered. Jonah knew that he'd update Ana on today's actions, but it was seeing Fawn that had Moses readily agreeing to ride to town.

"You're not fooling me, Moses. I know why you're riding back."

A toothy smile appeared, "Well, somebody has to keep the women informed."

Jonah inquired, raising an eyebrow with his disdainful look, "Nothing more on your mind?"

"Should some extra comfort and reassurance be needed, I'd be a poor man not to fulfill that need to the best of my ability."

Jonah smiled, "Just be sure it's the right woman you're providing comfort to, you devil."

Moses gave a mock salute, touching the brim of his hat with an open palm.

When Jonah arrived at the makeshift dining area, the old one having been knocked about by the British cannon balls, he found

Jackson already seated and being lectured about the worth of saving New Orleans.

Mike Benton was standing to one side. Seeing Jonah, he gave a look that implied…windbag. He then whispered, "This has been going on ten minutes already."

That the man was a very opinionated individual was quickly realized. "I tell you, Andy," the man started. It was easy to see that Jackson did not like being so addressed by a man who was not a close friend. "For New Orleans to be overwhelmingly Catholic," the man continued, "the population seems laissez-faire at best. The locals' favorite pastimes are gambling, drinking, and keeping Negro mistresses for their exotic sexual desires."

Hmm, I wonder how he knows that, Jonah thought.

"The streets are muddy and filth strewn. Why, sir, pirates freely roam the streets and associate with the upper class citizens. They'd have been hung at home."

This caused Jonah to wonder where home was. The man had a distinct Southern drawl, at times sounding 'put on'. *Hope he isn't from Georgia*, Jonah thought to himself.

The man continued on with his story, "I found the locals stubbornly refusing to detour from buying cheap contraband, so much so, that the real merchants can't make a living."

Ah, now we're getting to the meat of it, Jonah thought. He must have smirked out loud as Captain Lieupo elbowed him in the ribs and frowned at him.

"It's no wonder these plantation owners live in exorbitant luxury. They've grown rich on cotton and sugar. It's these…these moneyed gentry, who support the damnable pirates the most. I've no doubt most of their deals are made at that LaFitte fellow's stronghold." He then went too far in his tirade, "In truth, Andy, I was truly saddened to see one of those louts walking out as I walked in."

Everyone in the room held their breath. Jackson rose up from his chair, "That lout you speak of, sir, is Dominique Youx. He's never been charged or accused of being a pirate."

That might be stretching it a bit, Jonah thought, but he did not utter a word.

"Mr. Youx and his men are excellent gunners. I would not hesitate to say his battery was responsible for a significant amount of the destruction suffered today by our duel. Furthermore, I feel most blessed to have such a man with so much…naval experience. Now, Mr. Fargo, I'm not sure how gentlemen settle insults in your part of the country, but in Tennessee, one would seek satisfaction. Should you like to now address Mr. Youx, I will send…" Jackson paused and looked around the room. His eyes settled on Jonah. "I'll send Mr. Lee to bring back Mr. Youx. You can then make your comments and thoughts plain to Mr. Youx. Are you experienced with the pistol or blade, Mr. Fargo? I'm sure Mr. Youx would be fair, and since you're not from here, he would allow you your choice of weapon. Mr. Lee, would you fetch Mr. Youx?"

"Yes sir, General," Jonah replied.

"There's no need to, sir, I may have been a bit hasty repeating comments that I'd heard in New Orleans." This was said with Fargo looking at one of the governor's aides. "The time has certainly slipped away from me, General. I must take my leave."

As Fargo made his hurried departure, Jackson looked about the room. "I'll not have a brave soldier's character called into question. Not while I'm, Andy 'by God' Jackson." Jackson put the emphasis on 'Andy'.

Colonel Butler spoke first, "I was hoping he'd leave and not ruin our supper. We've had precious little today."

Jackson smiled as he sat back down and nodded to the orderly that he was ready to eat. He then looked at Jonah, "You knew that I was joking about fetching Dominique, didn't you?"

"Wasn't sure, General, but Mr. Fargo didn't think you were joking and that's what counts."

"Right as always, Jonah," Jackson responded.

THE SCOUTS REPORTED BACK to Jackson just before he turned in for the night. Henry Parrish and Scrap had gotten close enough to hear a captain talking to his sergeant. Apparently, they'd lost most of their gun crew. The captain was trying to make the sergeant understand that it was the engineers who had recommended using hogsheads filled with sugar as a means of cover and protection for the Redcoat gunners. 'Bloody fools,' the sergeant fumed. 'I lost most of the gunners in my battery. The ball went straight through them, killing every man. What were the idiots thinking?' 'That's enough, Sergeant,' the captain said, irritated at the sergeant's language when speaking of officers. 'It's not, Captain, begging your pardon for speaking plainly, but what are you going to tell the general if we're unable to put enough parts together to make a cannon. You've got no artillery men, they're dead… dead, damn those fools for engineers. I lost some good soldiers.' 'We can train some more,' the captain replied meekly. 'Not bloody likely,' the sergeant replied.

"After that they walked off so's we couldn't hear," Scrap said, with Henry agreeing.

The Halls were a bit later reporting in, but in time to hear Scrap and Henry talking about piecing cannons together. "That's what they's doing, General. Scavenger squads are out trying to get enough parts to make a gun. They ain't happy none," Tim said. "Seems the officer had those believing the British guns would all but destroy the Americans, so there'd be little resistance once the soldiers marched. One sodjer boy said he was bloody tired, bloody hungry, and about bloody ready to change sides. It 'peared like our boys had plenty to eat and a good place to sleep."

"That's disheartening for them but good for us," Jackson responded, smiling at this information. "They've had their assaults foiled twice now. Their artillery is basically gone. Our sharpshooters are picking off their sentinels," Jackson was saying to Colonel Butler and General Coffee when Donnie Hall interrupted him.

"Our Redskin brothers are at it now, General. I heard two shots, and you know them devils don't miss."

Jackson smiled at Hall, "Smith heard a sentinel telling his corporal the muskets didn't scare him like the hatchets did." He continued on, "No, we have about beaten down the British; poor conditions, poor food, no rest, and losing men. All we have to do," Jackson said, looking directly at Coffee, "is sit tight until we're looking at them in the eyes. We'll then open up."

Butler cleared his throat causing Jackson to say, "Yes, Colonel?"

"Things do appear to be going our way, sir, but let me remind the general that the British still have between twenty and thirty big guns while we have but sixteen. Their weight of metal is superior, as are their numbers."

Nobody spoke for a minute, and then Tim muttered, "Didn't do them much good today."

Smiling, Jackson stood up from the tiny table he was sitting behind. "By the Almighty, son, you are right. Hear that, Colonel? Our men have the spirit. This battle will not be lost, we will be victorious."

Mike Benton, who had been over to one side finishing some sketches by the lamplight, couldn't help but smile. *There was no back up in General Andrew Jackson.*

CHAPTER TWENTY EIGHT

During the night of January 1, 1815, insult was added to the gloom the British army had suffered that day. A cold rain had started to fall, and shivering wet men gathered around sizzling campfires with sodden blankets, trying to keep warm. Scouts reported to Jackson that Redcoat soldiers refused to drag a gun battery to safety, until General Pakenham showed up to personally issue the order.

The next few days were uneventful. Jonah, Richard Smith, and Mike Benton made their way back to New Orleans the next day which was January 2nd. After Jonah and Ana spent an hour together, she put on a dress and Mike Benton started to fulfill his bargain with Jonah to do her portrait. He had taken the hour to eat a good meal and put on clean clothes.

Seeing Benton, Ana wrinkled her nose at Jonah, "You could take in Mr. Benton's example and get cleaned up, Jonah."

Jonah made to sniff his armpits, only to have Ana throw her fan at him. Excusing himself, he called for bath water and drank another cup of coffee while he waited.

Toward noon, Benton was still at his painting, so Jonah strolled into the kitchen. He took a biscuit under the watchful eye of the cook and, breaking it open, he placed a sausage link between the halves.

"Mmm, this is good," Jonah said, and kissed the cook on the cheek.

"You better stay outta my kitchen. You ain't no better than that heathen, Moses, thinkin' you can charm yo way 'round me. I'm wise to yo devilment."

She could say what she wanted, but Jonah could tell she was pleased. "Mmm," he said again. "I'm liable to leave Ana here and take you back to Georgia with me."

The cook, smiling wide now, said, "Get yo' self another biscuit and get on outta heah. Yo ain't fooling nobody wid yo' sly ways."

Hearing a horse ride up in the courtyard, Jonah looked out. It was Captain Steve Lieupo. "Is everything quiet?" Jonah asked.

"As quiet as a church mouse," his friend replied. "Scouts say the Redcoats are still licking their wounds, but there's talk of reinforcements coming in."

"Are they ours or theirs?" Jonah inquired. Over two thousand Kentuckians were expected, but so far, they'd not been seen.

"The British," Lieupo replied. "Twenty-five hundred or more soldiers, under General Lambert. Jackson figures the British will stay put until the reinforcements get here. They'll make a big concerted effort then to fight us. Scouts say the Navy is constantly sending boats with food and other supplies. We've taken a few pot shots to discourage them a mite, but nothing to make a difference."

NOTHING HAPPENED ON JANUARY 2nd or 3rd. Jonah was able to spend time with Ana, in between her sittings with Benton. At lunch on the 2nd and dinner on the 3rd they ventured out for meals. Each time they invited a guest. Benton went to lunch but begged off the evening meal on the third.

Ana whispered that night in bed, "Mike probably went to see Miss Earles tonight."

"It would have to be a woman to tear him away from that meal," Jonah said, half-jokingly, only to get an elbow in the ribs for his comment. "God, what a boney elbow," he groaned. This got him another nudge. "You have to admit," Jonah said, "a big bowl of grits with boiled shrimp, sausage cooked to a crisp and layered around the edge of the bowl, with a gumbo filled with crawfish in the center of the grits. Mmm, I can't think of a thing that could tear me away from that."

"I can," Ana replied, being coy.

"What?"

"You'll see in time."

"That's just like a woman, always using your wiles on helpless men, trying to come between a man and his stomach."

On the 4th of January, word came to Jonah as he and Moses were saddling their horses. British General Lambert and twenty-seven hundred men, fresh and ready to fight, were at Lake Borgne. As soon as one scout had brought the news, another one followed with word that General Pakenham had ordered them brought up Bayou Bienvenue.

"Looks like the time is neigh for the British to make their move," Moses said.

Jonah nodded, "I told Ana we'd likely be back tonight. Let me go tell her things have changed."

Again Moses nodded his head. Both of them knew that the next few hours may be their last. Another twenty-seven hundred was a lot of reinforcement. *God will have to be on our side*, Moses thought. He started to go back inside, but instead brushed the morning dew aside on a cast iron patio chair and sat down. Ignoring the wetness to the seat of his pants, Moses sat in the quiet solitude. He'd had few regrets in his life, partly because of his relationship with the Lee's and partly because he held a deep abiding faith in the Almighty to see him through life's hazards. He could always remember Colonel Lee telling him and Jonah, 'Always be ready to meet your maker.' He'd innocently asked, "Are you ready, Colonel?" 'Yes, I am,' came the quick reply. 'I'm not raring to go, but I'm ready.'

The upcoming battle did not create a lot of fear. He and Jonah had faced death too many times, not that he didn't take caution when he was able. Only a fool would do that. He'd heard a man say, 'You ain't going until it's you time.' Well, he'd dispute that. He'd seen more than a few die suddenly from a careless act. It was their time, maybe, but had they not presented such a fine target, they may have prolonged things a bit. No, he believed you might have a set time based on the Lord's will, but there was some that had rushed it. Like the colonel said, he'd be ready but he'd take caution so more than likely he'd see the sunrise the next day. Hearing a door shut, Moses looked up.

It was the artist, Mike Benton. "Jonah told us of the scouting reports. He and Ana wanted a few minutes together. The painting is basically done, so I decided to ride back out with the two of you."

"You ever draw a picture of a black man?" Moses asked.

"A portrait, no I haven't, but a painting yes. Let me show you a couple of them." Benton opened a pad and thumbed through it a bit and then handed it to Moses.

"That's me," Moses said surprised. "Am I that ugly?"

"I would call it fierce," Benton replied. "Continue on."

The next page was Jonah, Moses, Richard Smith, and Scrap standing around a fire. The light from the fire shining on their faces while the rest of their bodies, though visible, were somewhat of a shadow because of the fog and the last one was just a charcoal sketch of him sitting on a wrought iron bench.

"You just did this one," Moses said, surprised.

Reading Moses' unspoken question, Benton spoke, "From the kitchen window. I saw you sitting here alone, under these huge oaks…"

"With a wet behind," Moses interrupted him.

Benton laughed, "I didn't include your bottom side, you'll notice."

"I'd love to buy this," Moses said. "I want to give it to Mama Lee."

"It's yours. Go put it up somewhere and I'll add a bit to it…ah… later." Benton paused a second and then took out the other sketches. "They need a bit more before I'll be satisfied with them, but if they go to the front they could get damaged."

Moses stood up and took them to his room. When he got back, Jonah was waiting with Ana. The two embraced and Jonah hurriedly climbed into the saddle. Benton handed Jonah his art pad and other tools all crammed into a small case, so that he could mount his horse. Moses hugged Ana, who gave him a kiss on the cheek.

"Be careful. I'll pray for you...all of you," she said.

Hmm, other than Mama Lee, that's the first time any woman has said she'll be praying for me. Dang, makes you feel good, Moses thought.

UNLIKE THE USUAL CANTER to the line, today Jonah and his comrades galloped. They reined in and turned their horses over to one of Jackson's orderlies. They spotted Jackson toward the front line. His orderly, Billy, was walking behind the general leading his horse, should he be needed quickly. The lawyer, Mr. Livingston, and artillery Captain Humphrey were walking with the general. They seemed to have stopped at Dominique Youx's battery. Jonah saw Youx hand Jackson a cup of coffee. The smell, that wonderful aroma of Cajun coffee, could already be appreciated and they were still twenty yards away.

"Hope he's got more," Benton mentioned.

"Me and you both," Moses added.

As they got nearer, Jackson could be heard saying, "That coffee smells better than what we can get, Youx," he said. "Where did you get such fine coffee? You smuggled it, maybe?" Jackson said, smiling as he lifted the cup to his mouth.

Dominique returned the smile, "Maybe so, General."

Jonah and his friends were near now and must have been spotted as Dominique handed Jonah a cup...one cup. The coffee was black as midnight. *Must be the last of the pot,* Jonah thought. He took a good sip and passed it to Benton, who sipped and gave it to Moses, who finished it with gusto.

"Did you hear our Kentuckians are here?" Jackson asked Jonah.

"No, sir only that the Redcoats' reinforcements had arrived."

Jackson nodded and continued, "We got nearly twenty four hundred Kentucky militiamen. Most of them need clothes and are half-starved, but that's not the worst of it," Jackson snapped. "Only seven hundred of them have guns." Jonah was totally dismayed. "I've sent Captain Lieupo and Richard Smith to persuade the mayor to release the muskets from the city armory. It should be of some help, if they're not too dusty to shoot."

Jonah looked at Jackson and asked, "Do you think he'll release them?" Jackson's look said it all.

"He'll release them or be shot," Livingston threw out.

Jackson and his entourage walked away, Captain Reid, who had walked up and heard the conversation, leaned over and whispered, "Jackson said not to come back without the guns. That's the reason he sent Richard Smith. He knew he'd brook no refusal."

"Do you think he'd shoot the mayor?" Benton asked.

"Aye...I've had it of mind a few times myself," Dominique answered. *He wouldn't 'less he had to*, Jonah thought, *but if it comes to it, he doubted Smith wouldn't do as ordered.*

"It won't be long now," Dominique said. "Choctaws are picking off some every now and then. You'll hear a shot every little bit. When the wind pushes the fog a bit, you can see the Redcoats lining up in formation."

Jonah glanced at his watch and realized it ought to have been broad daylight, but the fog was so dense, you couldn't see more than thirty or forty yards. Since the first of January, Jackson had kept the men busy. The redoubts were finished, and here and there a small fire was built to help with the chill. The fog wet the men's clothes and the chilly morning penetrated their damp clothes. Between the fog and smoke from the smoldering fires, the men along the line looked almost like ghosts.

"Eerie ain't it," Moses said, looking down the line.

"It'll clear in an hour or so," Dominique predicted.

One shot and then another was heard, but no return fire. "Choctaws," Beluche volunteered.

Later, the wind picked up and pushed the fog toward the Redcoat camp.

"Look," one of Youx's men shouted.

It was still somewhat dim but the British could be seen, hundreds of them. When Dominique didn't have his men raise up, Jonah asked politely, "Is it still to foggy to fire?"

"They're six hundred or six hundred and fifty yards off. We'll see if the fog clears a bit more and then we'll have us a war. You help with the ball and powder today…eh, Jonah. You help goot last time."

"We'll be glad to if Jackson doesn't send us elsewhere."

Dominique only nodded as his men spoke with excited voices. Up and down the line, men were lining up at the redoubt. One man was asleep on a cotton bale that had been broken open. A friend nudged him over with his foot, as he rolled onto the ground, a jug could be seen.

"To ward off the cold," Moses said.

It was cold, and as the wind picked up the temperature dropped. Somewhere down the line, in the direction they had just ridden from, a cannon fired.

"Old General Fleaujeac," Dominique said. "That's his six pounder. He served under Napoleon."

Jonah had come to realize there was a huge French population, not only in New Orleans, but all over Louisiana. Ana had met several French ladies since they had been in the city. *Would she be as happy in Thunderbolt and Savannah*, he wondered.

Suddenly, the stillness was gone. Thunder filled the air and the ground shook. Some of the British guns were invisible due to the fog, but the flash…the flame belching forth was plain and then suddenly there in the fog…a rainbow.

"It's the smoke and spent powder creating the hue," Youx said.

CHAPTER TWENTY NINE

A RIDER CAME TROTTING DOWN the line on his horse. "Every man with a long rifle to the firing line, and pick off every officer you see."

"They won't like that," a voice said. Turning they saw that it was Richard Smith, along with Scrap, Donnie and Tim Hall.

"Reckon we got here in time to have some fun," Donnie said. "Bet I get the first ossifer."

Bang...a long rifle went off and you could see a riderless horse galloping off. "You done lost that bet," Tim advised.

"I was talking about our group," Donnie replied. "Can't expect me to pick off ones I can't see." The last was shouted as the air was rent with the sound of cannons.

Back and forth the great guns fired. Still the British kept coming. The Redcoats seemed to ignore the ball and grape that slammed into their ranks as quick as the cannons could be loaded. More officers were now seen. Donnie threw up his long gun...bang. An officer tumbled from his saddle. Everywhere more rifles cracked and officers fell. The British line halted. They were trained to face the cannon, but they'd never seen a time when in five minutes, the entire front of the formation was without a single officer. Most of them were dead on the fog and dew soaked ground.

"We've been in battles in the northwest with Harrison," Jonah told Smith, "but I don't ever remember seeing anything like this."

In ten minutes time, the entire leading battalion was practically destroyed. As the leading battalion had advanced with ladders to climb the ramparts, soon those that survived the withering fire of cannons and backwoods' marksmanship threw down their burden and ran for their lives. The next column moved up then. No doubt they were nervous and scared. *I'd be*, Jonah thought.

Amidst the firing, somebody shouted, "Thems the 93rd Highlanders, see their kilts."

As the Americans fired their cannons and rifles, the 93rd disintegrated. The general leading the regiment was shot off his horse and several of his men rushed to him. Still the Highlanders advanced; in the face of terrible losses they kept coming.

"My rifle barrel is so hot, I'm scairt to shoot it," Scrap swore.

Jonah looked over at his friend. Scrap's face was blackened from all of the smoke. He called a water boy over and poured a gourd dipper full of water down his gun barrel. He then took another dipper full and drank deep. "Set that bucket down and fetch another one," Scrap told the boy.

A shout went up. Jonah watched as another British general's head seem to just explode. Four bullets had smashed into General Gibbs. Seeing the general fall, the British Commander, General Pakenham, watched as his Redcoat soldiers started to falter. He mounted a horse and charged to the front of the line. He called to the Highlanders to follow him. As he regrouped his men and rode forward, grapeshot shattered his knee and killed his horse.

"What a brave man," Moses said.

"A fool," Scrap swore. No sooner were the words out of Scrap's mouth, than the general was struck again and toppled off the back of his horse.

Another officer tried to gather what was left of the men. As he charged, he was shot dead, as were most of his men.

Suddenly, a rider rushed up, "The Creoles have turned tail and run. We need reinforcements. Colonel William Thornton, a British colonel, has crossed the river with four hundred and fifty men. Seeing them, the Creoles with their loud-mouthed general ran, as did the two hundred Kentuckians that Jackson sent to reinforce them."

"They'd not have run if Colonel Richard Mentor Johnson had been their commander," Jonah swore.

"Neither would they have run if Captain Gesslin had been around," Moses added.

As reinforcements went to counter the British assault, they came upon Commodore Patterson. "Damn cowards," he roared. "We had to abandon our guns."

The men slowly advanced now. Backwoodsmen slipped from tree to tree. Jonah rushed up to a gnarled oak tree and waited for Moses. *We should have met up with the Redcoats by now,* Jonah thought. Someone whistled…it was a Choctaw. Like shadows, they pushed forward. They were now at an empty clearing. A Choctaw ran up to them, and pointing across the river, he said, "In boat. They've broke it off."

"Wonder why?" Donnie said.

"They must have been recalled," Jonah answered. "No other reason, all those men and some of the navy guns. They could have made life a bit more difficult. They were called back for reinforcement, most likely."

Moses felt a chill, and his body gave a shudder. "Divine intervention, I'd call it," he said. "The Lord was with us this day." Several of the men muttered their agreement.

"We best leave a couple of the Indians to bring word if the Redcoats head back this way. In the meantime, let's go see what the general has in mind," Jonah said.

"Good idea," someone in the group said, as they started back to camp.

During the lull, stretcher bearers were running here and there, picking up the wounded that lay behind the redoubt.

"Give me a hand here," Dominique Youx asked Jonah and Moses.

They could see several of Youx's men with light wounds, but two of the men had been hit hard. One man's leg was held by a small amount of muscle. The bone was shattered and pieces of jagged bone were showing. A tourniquet was wrapped around the man's leg, and someone had given him a bottle of rum. Someone had fetched a door to use as a stretcher. As they neared the surgical area of the field hospital, a fire had been built. The glows of red hot cauterizing irons were very visible and the stench of burning flesh was in the air.

A woman, maybe a nurse or just a volunteer saw them and directed them inside the surgical tent. The first thing they saw was a surgeon cauterizing a bloody stump. The man was strapped to the table, yet orderlies were still holding onto the man's shoulders as the iron was applied. The man's screams were quieted and now he just lay there and moaned.

"If the shock doesn't kill him, he'll have a good chance to survive," the surgeon muttered.

The nurse who led them in put a sponge in a bucket of bloody water and wiped off an operating table. A chunk of someone's flesh was tossed into a tub containing arms and legs, or as it was labeled, 'wings and limbs'.

As the men transferred the wounded gunner from the door to the table an orderly picked up some dirty, bloody instruments and sloshed clean water on them. He then took a bottle of whiskey, took a swig, and poured the rest over the instruments.

The surgeon walked over and, seeing their gaze, he said, "It's the only antiseptic we have."

None of the men knew what he meant, but when the gunner had his pants cut away, another bottle appeared and half the bottle's contents were poured over the wound. *Something to clean it*, Jonah thought. The gunner was allowed another pull from his rum bottle. After that, the tissue holding the leg on was cut away. The bone was then sawed off clean and some shorter. The gunner clinched on a leather strap but did not utter a sound. Sweat covered his forehead and his eyes were shut tight.

In less than two minutes, the surgeon called for an iron. He put the red hot iron to the stump. This time the gunner rose up and screamed and fell back unconscious. The surgeon ignored the scream and went about his job.

The nauseating smell of burning flesh filled the air. When he was satisfied with his work, the surgeon loosened the tourniquet and touched a few bleeders, cauterizing them. He then poured more whiskey over the wound and sewed up a flap he'd made to cover the bone. When he was finished, the orderlies took the gunner to another tent.

Forty people were already there in the recovery tent. No beds were available, so the wounded were placed on straw pallets. Nurses walked around giving water and checking dressings. At one pallet, a nurse called out, "We've a dead man here."

Was that how it was? Jonah wondered. *No feelings, no apparent sorrow.*

Moses whispered, "They must get used to it."

"They have to," Tim said. "They see it all the time."

"I hope when I go it's quick," Donnie said.

"You and me both," Jonah agreed.

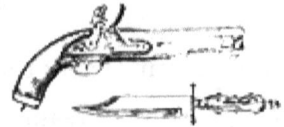

CHAPTER THIRTY

THE BATTLE SMOKE AND some remnants of fog lingered. Jonah and his fellow stretcher bearer went back along the line now. The misty field of battle they saw was strewn with wounded, dying, and dead men. Henry Parrish walked up and swore, "Worser 'n' Horseshoe Bend."

The murderous fire from the Americans along their thick barricade of earth proved too much for the Redcoats. There wasn't a single British soldier who climbed over the earthworks. Several had died in the bloody ditches. The only real concern had been Colonel Thornton's route of the Creoles and Kentuckians. They were now back across the river with the Choctaws and backwoodsmen volunteers making their life miserable as they retreated.

Jackson with his staff now walked from one end to the other of his earthworks. One man shouted, "We can still take it to 'em, Andy."

Jackson replied, "If they want it, let 'em come to us."

Men soaked with sweat and grime, with faces blackened from the gunsmoke, cheered their leader. It was a proud moment.

"Andy 'by God' Jackson knew what he was doing when we built the dirt barricades," one man swore, only to have another man add, "Don't forget about him flooding the fields so they'd have to traipse in the mud."

"Hip, hip, hooray," another cheer went up.

Captain Lieupo hesitated as Jackson walked off, "You know that only about half of our men got to fire a shot. In some places they shot, and then let another man shoot while they reloaded."

Jackson was now talking to Dominique Youx, "I was watching in my glass, Mr. Youx, and I noticed those pretty Redcoats and imposing Highlanders in their entire military array, quickly vanished. I believe what's left of them are concealing themselves behind the shrubbery or lying in ditches and gullies."

It was now Dominique's gunners who started another cheer. *They can cheer*, Jonah thought, but it was the painful cries, the shrieks, and writhing wounded that held his attention. *What a waste*, he thought.

Standing beside him, Moses was feeling the same emotions, "At least it ain't us. Jackson knew what he was doing. There ain't a man there what remembers the backbreaking hours with the pick and spade." Jonah nodded, no need for words, not with Moses.

Little did Jackson and the Americans realize how beaten the British were. While Colonel Thornton had some success with his assault, he was severely wounded. They had killed one American and wounded five others, while his forces had lost one hundred twenty-five killed and wounded. With the death of General Pakenham, General Lambert was placed in command. When he learned of his army's losses, he was stunned. The number of dead among the higher grade officers was frightful. The British had lost three major-generals, eight colonels and lieutenant colonels, six majors, eighteen captains, and fifty-four subalterns.

During the lull, Jackson sent General Humbert, an officer from the French Revolutionary Expedition to Ireland in 1798, to take that which the Creoles had abandoned. Richard Smith and Henry Parrish went along as scouts. Their orders…return to New Orleans, ferry across the river and march down to where they could meet the enemy and drive them from the lines.

At midday, a party of British soldiers was seen approaching. Major Sir Harry Smith, aide-de-camp to General Lambert, was accompanied by a trumpeter and a soldier bearing a white flag. Jackson sent Colonel Butler to meet the British. Jonah and Captain Lieupo accompanied him. After an exchange of courteous salutations, Major Smith handed Colonel Butler a letter. Butler handed the letter to Captain Lieupo.

Captain Lieupo opened and read the letter, "General Lambert proposes an armistice of twenty-four hours, so that the dead and wounded can be removed from the field." He saluted and hurriedly took the letter to Jackson.

Jackson, unaware of Pakenham's death, and realizing that General Humbert had not had time to cross the river and regain the west bank, sent back a reply that he was ready to 'treat' with the commander-in-chief of the British army. He further stated that it was a matter of surprise to him that the letter he had received was not directly from that officer.

"I would bet, sir, that General Pakenham has been killed," Jonah advised. "I know he went down after he received a hail of grape from Youx's battery. He was carried from the field."

"You are probably right, Jonah, but I want the British to acknowledge this. It will also give General Humbert the time to cross the river and therefore, from a diplomatic sense, be considered crossed."

That's Jackson, always thinking, seeking the advantage, Jonah thought.

In half an hour, the British major returned with the same proposal but it was signed, John Lambert, Commander-in-Chief of the British Forces. Jackson agreed to an armistice but stipulated on the eastern bank only, that hostilities were not to be suspended on the western bank of the river. He went on to include neither party should send reinforcements until the end of the armistice.

Cunning but not unfair, Jonah thought. Later, he learned that the British had already sent reinforcements. Receiving Jackson's note, General Lambert asked for time to consider Jackson's request. He would send a definite reply by ten o'clock on the morrow.

In the meantime, Jonah said to those around him, "Men who might have been saved will perish."

The cannons again thundered forth. They were answered with a will until around two in the afternoon.

British General Lambert, not wanting to be duped by Jackson, sent a British officer over to the west bank to inspect the works on that shore. When he returned, he gave the depressing news that the position could not be held with less than two thousand men. Reluctantly, General Lambert sent an order to the commander on the west bank, Colonel Gubbins to abandon his position and come back across the river. General Humbert's men and those who had run now joined forces and pressured the Redcoats with fire until they crossed over the river.

Commodore Patterson and General Morgan then occupied their redoubts again. During the night, Patterson's sailors bored out the spikes of guns that they'd abandoned, so that they'd be ready to strengthen their line come tomorrow.

The dead Redcoats in front of Jackson's lines, meanwhile, lay scattered and heaped upon one another. Many of the wounded could be seen crawling in agony back to their lines, while the Americans let them go. Other British soldiers lingered in agony. One man was in such agony that Jonah spoke to his friends and they went over the redoubts and pulled the soldier out of the ditch and took him to the surgeon. Seeing their efforts, several others followed suit and several of the British wounded were even taken into New Orleans to be cared for.

Little did the Americans know that General Lambert had only two regiments left. Lambert conferred with Admiral Cochrane at a nearby plantation house; Admiral Cochrane urged a renewed attack, but he'd not seen the shape of the army. He'd not witnessed the accuracy of the American backwoodsmen with their long rifles. To attack such a position was murder, nothing less. Disagreeing with Cochrane, Lambert walked out.

They now realized Pakenham's assault of Jackson's line had cost over three thousand three hundred men. Eight hundred and twenty-eight were dead and nearly two thousand five hundred were wounded. Jackson, meanwhile, had lost only eight men killed and fourteen wounded.

"The unerring hand of Providence shielded my men," Jackson told his people.

For the next ten days not a shot was fired at the front. Jonah felt that it was over. He said as much to Jackson, who sent out scouts.

"They are withdrawing, General," Richard Smith reported. "They are short on boats to transport them so it's taking a while."

Jonah spent most nights at the Hotel Provincial with Ana. Occasionally, they would dine out with friends. Mike Benton finished Ana's portrait. He also gave Jonah a group of sketches he'd put together on one painting. One was of Jonah and Ana eating Christmas dinner with Jackson.

Sickness soon began to run through the Americans. Sick men, yellow and gaunt, were carried into hospitals. Influenza, fever and dysentery killed over five hundred men. Some had stood at their posts too weak to move and had just laid down and died.

On the 18th of January, an exchange of prisoners was held with military order. Greeted by comrades, friends, and family, the prisoners, down to the last one, stated that they had been treated most appropriately by the British.

THE FOLLOWING MORNING THE sun was high without a cloud. There was no fog or rain and the sun had burned away any chill. Jackson was talking to Jonah, Moses, the Halls, and Scrap. He desired a reconnoiter of the British camp. He was giving his instructions when he was interrupted by Captain Lieupo.

"General, Dr. Wadsdale, the British medical officer, is here to see you. He has a letter from General Lambert."

The letter advised Jackson that he was in fact departing. General Lambert related that he had eighty wounded men, who out of necessity, had to be left behind. He pleaded to the humanity of Jackson to care for the men.

Jackson readily agreed to the care of the wounded men but was cautious to not rush out to the abandoned camp. A party of Hinds' Dragoons was assigned to the task to reconnoiter the camp.

Seeing Jonah, Hinds called to him, "You were with us when they landed, you want to ride with us as we pester them back to their ships."

Jonah was about to decline when Jackson said, "Go ahead. You can tell Madison that you watched them all the way to the sea."

After Hinds' Dragoons left, Major Villere, who had discovered the British landing, was sent to scour the woods for any remnant of Redcoats. Jackson then visited the wounded British soldiers and promised them he'd see to their care.

THE 23ʀᴅ ᴏꜰ Jᴀɴᴜᴀʀʏ was appointed a day of thanksgiving, for the Lord's Providence. It was a day of great celebration. Jackson sent an invitation to Jonah to ride with his officers when they made their entrance to the square. He had started to decline, but because of Ana he accepted the invitation and rode just to the right of Jackson as they made their entrance.

After a long day of celebration, Jonah enjoyed a nightcap and spoke to Ana, "Tomorrow I will finish my dispatches to the president and then we'll make preparations to go home."

"Home," Ana repeated. "It sounds so good. What will your parents think of me? A kept woman all these many months."

"They'll think nothing of it. We won't mention it and they won't ask."

"How will we get home?" Ana asked.

"It has to be decided, Dominique Youx has promised passage should we desire it, so we'll talk to him about it tomorrow."

EPILOGUE

THE NEXT TWO WEEKS went by quickly. Victory balls and celebrations happened almost nightly. They soon became tiresome. Ana seemed to enjoy them, but even she grew tired. General Jackson had been present at a ball at the Lawyer Livingston's home. At this celebration, somebody declared that Andy 'by God' Jackson needed to run for President. Jackson tried to curtail this talk but, bowing to Ana, he stated in front of the entire room of guests, that if he were to ever seek such a high office, he would only do so if Jonah Lee agreed to become a presidential advisor for him as he had been for Madison. This brought a lot of applause. Jonah had become somewhat of a celebrity as the President's man here in New Orleans and at Horseshoe Bend in Alabama.

Someone asked, "What about it, Jonah?"

Pausing a second to collect his thoughts, Jonah took a swallow of his brandy. "I would only have two considerations," he said. "First, if my future bride," saying this Jonah indicated Ana, "were to consent." Applause broke out again with a few here...here's. "Second, only if my brother were welcome as well. I rarely go far without Moses." This time there was a polite applause, but nothing like the first energetic response.

Most everyone recognized Moses, the half Indian, half black child taken in and raised as a brother to Jonah by the Lees. His acceptance in New Orleans could be taken for granted, but in Washington, D.C., the nation's capital. That might be different. However, anyone who knew Jonah, from President Madison to General Jackson and those present, knew Jonah meant what he said. If Moses was not a part of it, then there'd be no Jonah.

Mike Benton was showing some of his battlefield art to an appreciative crowd when Carolyn Meeks, the wife of lawyer Edward Meeks, who was an associate of Livingston, tapped Jonah on the shoulder.

"Yes, Madam."

"You have a visitor waiting in the foyer."

I wonder who this could be, Jonah thought as he walked to see his guest. "By all that's holy," Jonah blasphemed. "Cooper Cain. Come in, my friend."

"I'm not appropriately dressed," Cooper replied.

"You look good to me," Jonah said, and taking his friend's arm, they walked back to where the guests were. Several turned and a number broke out in smiles as they recognized the latecomer. "Ladies and Gentlemen," Jonah spoke out. "We have the unexpected pleasure to make welcome my dear friend, who some of you know already. General Jackson and the rest of you fine people, it's my pleasure to introduce Captain Cooper Cain, of the privateer ship, *SeaFire*."

So this is Jonah's pirate friend, Ana thought. *Damned if he ain't something to look on. No wonder he has such a reputation.* She had heard Mrs. Meeks speaking of his manly charms, and who, as her partner at cards, had filled her purse considerably.

After introducing Cooper to Ana, he was then introduced to General Jackson, who made a big to-do about the civilian navy helping with supplies and keeping sea lanes open. Cooper next met Mike Benton. Before Jonah could really save him, Lawyer Livingston had Cooper in tow and he was whisked away. No doubt, Livingston was glad to see Cooper. If the good Colonel Lee was right, the lawyer was an investor in Cooper's privateer ship and had undoubtedly made a good return on his investment.

Jonah looked across the room at Dominique Youx, who for his part in the recent battles, was looked upon as something of a hero and celebrity. Jackson was part of the reason for this. In his victory speech, he gave appreciation for the brave men of Barataria, especially Dominique and his gunners.

When Ana and Jonah had a moment where they could speak, she whispered, "Your friend is not what I expected."

Jonah laughed, "You mean because he didn't have a peg leg, a patch over his eye, and say 'argh, matey, a handsome wench she be.'"

Ana punched Jonah on the arm good-naturedly, "You are terrible."

"Argh, matey, yer right." This earned Jonah another punch.

Ana then leaned in and whispered, "He is handsome in a way. Look at all the women who have gathered around him."

"Aye," Jonah said, still playing the pirate. "He could bed a wench or two, but Cooper is a one-woman man. He's only had two loves that I know of. One was killed by a former suitor, the other his present wife, Maddy. Did I tell you Maddy's father was a British admiral? Her brother is a naval, British Navy captain," Jonah corrected himself.

"One wife killed by a suitor, you said," Ana quizzed.

"That's a long story, something we'll discuss in private."

"That good, hmm," Ana replied, already expecting a juicy tale. Her future husband, it seemed, didn't have dull friends.

AFTER THE PARTY WAS over, Cooper rode back to Hotel Provincial with Jonah and Ana. They drank coffee and swapped stories until the wee hours and then retired. Jonah was expecting Ana to bring up Cooper's first wife. Instead, she pulled him close and whispered, "I love you," and fell immediately asleep.

At breakfast the next morning, introductions were made to Captain, now freshly promoted to Major, Steve Lieupo. Richard Smith was there and was introduced to Cooper as well. Moses hadn't shown up yet, but did just before noon. He and Fawn had been together most of the night. Moses had invited her to return to Georgia with them, but she liked New Orleans and didn't want to leave the city.

"I'm sorry," Jonah had started to say, but Moses waved it away.

"Oddly enough, I'm not. I have enjoyed Fawn immensely," Moses admitted. "But she's not willing to clean up her manners and I wouldn't introduce her to Mama Lee without her trying. So...we agreed to part ways. Speaking of Fawn, has anyone seen or heard from Lucy?"

Richard Smith smiled this time, "I think she's attached herself to Scrap." This did bring smiles to the group.

Cooper took Jonah aside and said, "I stopped off here to get rid of some contraband that had been obtained before the word was out that the war was officially over. When I saw the shape LaFitte's place was in, I figured the British did it. Then I find out that Patterson did it, the scoundrel."

"With the governor's blessing," Jonah added. "This, in spite of, pressure from numerous city leaders. Jackson even hinted that some of LaFitte's money should be returned. 'He was pardoned' was Claiborne's flat response."

"I'd like to get the sod to meet me with swords," Cooper swore. That Cooper Cain was a man of extraordinary skill with swords was common knowledge. Someone might agree to pistols but only a fool would face him with blades.

After talking, a decision was made to return back to Georgia with Cooper aboard the *SeaFire*. They would set sail within the week. Richard Smith and Major Lieupo would stay in New Orleans until they were relieved by Jackson, which would be a while yet. Rumor had it that Jackson was to be called before the court. *Good luck with that*, Jonah thought.

Donnie and Tim Hall thought they'd like to see what it was like being out to sea in a 'big boat.' Jonah explained that it was a ship, and not to call the *SeaFire* a boat in front of the crew. A lesson that he'd learned the hard way.

Farewells were made to Jackson, who asked Jonah to stay in touch, and he let him know that he expected an invitation to the wedding.

Jackson then became very serious. "You're a good man, Jonah, and you have the knack for making the right calls. You also have a keen eye of observation. I will always consider you a most trusted advisor... and a trusted friend. You will always be welcomed in my home or as a part of my staff. I have sent a letter to Madison expressing my grateful appreciation for your service."

Jonah was touched; he still couldn't help but notice though, the omission of the word...president. Would Jackson make a good president? Jonah wondered for a moment, and then decided: yes, in his own way, the warrior would be good for the nation, if somebody kept a tight rein on the man.

"WHAT A PRETTY SHIP," Ana declared as she cast her eyes on *SeaFire*. The ship had been anchored at Barataria. When it was decided that they'd return to Savannah with Cooper, Dominique Youx had a few of his men transport them in pirogues. The hotel's livery boy had finally made peace with Coco, so Ana gave the mule to the boy.

Packing up Ana's things took so many chests that it took two pirogues to get them to the ship.

"Seems like when we found her, she didn't have a single thing that wasn't on her back," Moses declared, only to get an elbow for his comment.

Jean LaFitte greeted them when they reached Barataria. "Please forgive our appearance," LaFitte apologized. "Things are not as they once were."

"You mean before the war," Ana said, not understanding about Patterson's viciousness.

Being a gentleman, Jean bowed and said, "Yes, before the war."

After getting everything loaded aboard the ship, Cooper explained that tomorrow he wished to visit a friend and, if they desired, they could all go over to meet Mrs. Cindy Veigh.

"Oh, I've met her," Ana beamed. "I'd love to go visit."

THE FIRST PERSON THEY met as they tied off at the tiny dock at Grand Isle was a young black teen that Cooper addressed as Jumper. "You are still staying away from the gators, I see," Cooper said.

"Yas, suh. Ain't no gator fast enough to get Jumper."

Hugs were given and the boy ran on up to the house to announce their guests. Cindy Veigh stood at the door; her hand was shielding her eyes from the sun. She was dressed nicely but not in the elaborate gown she'd been wearing when Ana had met her.

As Cindy and Cooper embraced, Jonah whispered, "This is where Cooper met his first wife."

After greeting Cooper, Cindy turned her attention to her other guests. "Jonah and Moses," she declared. "It's good to see you again." Recognizing Ana then, she said, "So this is the rogue you plan to marry?"

"Yes, Madam."

"Mimi," Cindy called. "Fetch us a pitcher of tea with ice and let's see, four...no five glasses. Jumper, you run tell Gus that Cooper is here. He'll likely want some cigars to take back with him." Cooper smiled and nodded at this comment. "Tell Belle that we have company for supper. She knows what Cooper likes." Cindy looked at Ana and explained, "Belle is Jumper's ma and Gus is his pa."

"Belle is the best cook in the world," Cooper said, and then added, "Just like Cindy is the prettiest woman in the world."

"It's full of it, you are," Cindy declared, but she said it with a smile.

Supper that night started with a cup of jambalaya, and then progressed to fried catfish, Belle's special grits, a cornbread like batter, that had whole corn in the mix and deep fried. After dinner was finished, Belle served up her beignets and poured cups of Café au lait.

Later, when the men went outside, Ana asked Cindy about Cooper's first wife.

"First you'll have to admit New Orleans is like no other place on earth," Cindy said. When Ana nodded, Cindy went on, "I'm sure you've heard some of the ladies talk about the Quadroon Ball."

"Oh yes," Ana said, thinking this was going to be juicy.

"Over the years slave owners have bed their slave women. When that woman is bedded, her children become less black and have more and more whiter features; until her black lineage is reduced further and further." Cindy went on to explain the difference between a mulatto, a quadroon, an octoroon, and so own. She continued, "The mothers of these girls start at an early age teaching them how to pleasure a man. I've heard it said the mothers teach the girls to be virtuous in the art of exotic sex. Every wealthy man is now basically expected to have one of these girls and most of them purchase contracts for their sons. A contract is made where the father agrees to purchase a nice house for the girl to live in, and the house is hers. She will receive a lifetime allowance and any offspring will be recognized and cared for."

"They must be really talented," Ana gasped.

"They are," Cindy replied, matter-of-factly. "Now wives of old men usually don't concern themselves with 'what they don't know.' A new wife, though, expects her husband to forget about any mistresses. Sophia was special; she was only one sixteenth black. She was an exotic beauty like no other I've ever seen. Her 'man' got married and was away for a while. He came back and found his brother trying to rape Sophia, and killed him. He was in truth very much in love with the girl. The father, Mister d'Arcy, had Sophia come stay with me until things quieted down. In the meantime, Cooper visited and it was love at first sight for the two of them. Eli Taylor, Cooper's captain, was able to secure a deal where Sophia's contract was bought. Cooper paid every cent of it...ten thousand dollars. They married and moved to Savannah. While Cooper was at sea, the d'Arcy son, by chance, happened to see her. He followed her to her hotel room and burst in. Sophia was trying to get away from d'Arcy, and fell over the balcony to her death. Young d'Arcy killed himself then in front of Eli Taylor. Cooper went half-crazy. It was only the chance meeting and later rescue of Maddy Anthony that saved him. A miracle from heaven, I called it. She was there at the right time, anyway. I've met her and think as much as I loved Sophia, I love Maddy even more. She calls Cooper 'Sir Pirate', and makes her daddy irate and her mama laugh. Her mother is from around Savannah, I believe."

THE SKY WAS CLEAR with puffy, lazy, white clouds overhead. The ship, *SeaFire*, moved along under full sail. Ana was thrilled by the sea and the wind. Everyone aboard ship had been so polite and kind.

"They'd better be, or I'll know why," a burly man named Diamond said.

"Aye," Spurlock agreed.

There was a tiny, little fellow called Banty, who was always around and very entertaining. Doctor Beau Cannington, the ship's doctor, was a pleasant man and he ate with them every evening. Ana hadn't realized that ships carried doctors aboard.

"Most don't, at least, not real doctors," Cooper said.

Every night straws were drawn and four crew members dined with the captain's special guests.

"Learn't him most what he knows," Banty bragged.

The Halls enjoyed the voyage as well. "Beats a horse," Tim said.

Ana wondered if Moses missed Fawn more than he admitted. She was able to engage him a few times in conversation, and once she explained how she looked forward to his being not just her brother-in-law, but her brother as well. "I've never had a brother, you know."

Finally, they sat at the dining table and Cooper announced that this would be their last evening at sea.

Johannes Ewers, a big burly German, said, "Aye. We drop anchor before noon tomorrow."

That night in their tiny cot, Ana snuggled close to Jonah, "I'm so glad you loved me enough to come after me."

"Did you doubt it?" Jonah asked.

"No, but I wasn't sure you'd still want me after..."

Jonah put his finger to her lips, "Shh, forget about that. Tomorrow we'll be home."

Home, Ana thought. *How good that sounded...home.*

HISTORICAL NOTES

I TRIED TO REMAIN AS true and as close to the actual events that took place during the Battle of New Orleans as possible. While the events leading to the battle are interspersed with filler, I did this to keep the book flowing.

From the first night the British touched American soil and Jackson's defeat of the British on January 8th, only three real actions took place. An enormous amount of time was spent waiting. Jackson took advantage of this and built an earth redoubt along the entire line of his eastern defense. A huge ditch was built that proved to be, along with the earthen redoubt, insurmountable.

Nearly twenty-five hundred men were killed and wounded in one charge. During the lull, between 'battles', Jackson's scouts, including his Choctaw Indians, reaped a terrible toll on the British sentinels. The American commanders instructing their sharpshooters to kill officers was something the British had never faced. The British Officer Corps were reduced to almost nothing in one day. Three British generals were killed in one battle.

For references I used three books on the War of 1812. For certain dates and specifics, I used the web. A little treasure I found was a book I downloaded titled, *'The Story of the Battle of New Orleans'*. This was written by Stanley C. Arthur, but I don't have a date. This story gave eyewitness accounts by officers and men from both sides. The language was such that it was probably written in the 1800's. It was published by the Louisiana Historical Society in 1915. My last source was *'The War of 1812, the Southern Theater'*.

The song: *The Battle of New Orleans* was a big hit for Johnny Horton in 1959. It was written by Jimmy Driftwood. My daddy used to sing it to me and I've sung it to my grandboys. They love the verse:

> We fired our cannons till the barrel melted down
> So we grabbed an alligator and we fought another round
> We filled his head with cannon balls –n- powdered his behind
> And when we touched the powder off, the gator lost his mind.

About the Author

Michael Aye is a retired Naval Medical Officer. He has long been a student of early American and British Naval history. Since reading his first Kent novel, Mike has spent many hours reading the great authors of sea fiction, often while being "haze gray and underway" himself. This is his third novel on the War of 1812.

Acknowledgements

Thanks to Chris and Jay, the good folks at Bitingduck, for continuing to work with me and bring my stories to print. You are a really great team, and I feel lucky to have you in my corner.

Greg Clark, your smile and energy is contagious. Thanks for lunch.

George, Jim, Alaric, and Bill, where would I be if it wasn't for old salts such as yourself willing to advise and answer my questions.

And especially, thanks to Pat, without her undying efforts there would be no Michael Aye novels. She is truly the glue that holds things together. Her name should be above mine.

www.ingramcontent.com/pod-product-compliance
Lightning Source LLC
Chambersburg PA
CBHW070740160426
43192CB00009B/1520